Looking at Teaching Through the Lens of the FFT Clusters

Study Guide
Set 8

Copyright © 2018 The Danielson Group. All rights reserved. ISBN: 978-1-947862-07-4

No part of this publication may be reproduced, distributed, or transmitted in any form or by any means, including photocopying, recording, or other electronic or mechanical methods, without the prior written permission of the publisher, except in the case of brief quotations embodied in critical reviews and certain other noncommercial uses permitted by copyright law. For permission requests, contact the publisher at the email address below.

The Danielson Group
contact@danielsongroup.org

Contents

Study Guide Overview
    Introduction 5
    Background. 5
    Contents of the Study Guides. 6
    Using the Study Guides. 8
    Post-Study Activities 11
    Connection to the Framework for Teaching Clusters. 12

ELA; Grade 4
    A Study Guide for Teacher Learning Communities 15
    Study Guide for Teachers Answer Key 29
    Study Guide for Instructional Coach Learning Communities 33
    Study Guide for Instructional Coach Answer Key 47
    Record of Evidence 51

ELA; Grade K
    A Study Guide for Teacher Learning Communities 69
    Study Guide for Teachers Answer Key 81
    Study Guide for Instructional Coach Learning Communities 85
    Study Guide for Instructional Coach Answer Key 99
    Record of Evidence 102

Math; Grade 9
    A Study Guide for Teacher Learning Communities 115
    Study Guide for Teachers Answer Key 126
    A Study Guide for Instructional Coach Learning Communities 129
    Study Guide for Instructional Coach Answer Key 142
    Record of Evidence 144

Appendix A: The FFT Clusters Study Guide Series Team 162

Appendix B: List of Study Guide Sets. 163

Study Guide Overview

Introduction

Welcome to the FFT (Framework for Teaching) series of Clusters Study Guides. Their purpose is to guide professioncommunities as they engage in activities and discussions to enhance their own practices and the practices of their colleagues. An Instructional Set of lesson artifacts (that may include lesson plans, a video of the entire lesson, student work, and teacher commentary) is used as a resource for each Study Guide. The combination of the Study Guide activities, the Instructional Set artifacts, and the user's experience yields a powerful method of examining teaching and applying learning to one's own practice.

Background

The Instructional Sets are actual lessons led by teachers with their own students. The videos run the duration of the lesson. The teachers and students are not actors, and the lessons are part of their curriculum, not something that was scripted for the Study Guides. The Danielson Group is extremely appreciative of the teachers and their students for providing an opportunity for others to view authentic classroom artifacts for the purpose of professional growth.

A team of educational practitioners and Danielson Group consultants, who have extensive experience in effective teaching practices and professional development training, created this Study Guide series (see Appendix A for the team members). The team received rigorous training on the FFT

Clusters and on how to analyze the teaching and learning evident in the Instructional Sets. They worked with Charlotte Danielson, lead consultants, and each other to create the contents of the Guides.

The series includes many Study Guides. Each Guide was written for a group of accompanying Instructional Sets. The collection includes a sampling of K–12 lessons in Mathematics, English Language Arts, Science, Social Studies, and Science Technology. The majority of lessons are in Mathematics and English Language Arts. Analyzing lessons from a variety of grades and subject areas provides opportunities for educators to stretch their analytic skills and enhance their understanding of the FFT Clusters. A list of the Instructional Sets can be found in Appendix B.

The team created a Record of Evidence for each Instructional Set. The activities portion of the Study Guide provides highlights of the Instructional Set, whereas the Record provides an extensive list of evidence gleaned from the video and artifacts for the FFT Clusters. A Record also includes interpretations of the evidence by the authors who were trained as coders. For each Record, two coders analyzed an Instructional Set independently, then compared their records to produce a composite version for the Study Guide. The Record of Evidence does not contain scores or evaluations, since the evidence is intended for use in professional conversations.

Contents of the Study Guides

Each Study Guide provides a multi-step process for examining the contents of an Instructional Set, reflecting on and discussing its contents, and applying learning from such study to new situations. Each Guide provides the following steps:

Step 1: Lesson Overview

This section provides a high-level summary of the lesson, culled from the video, lesson plans, and artifacts, to provide readers with some background information about the Instructional Set. Many include pre-observation notes in addition to the lesson plans. All lessons are based on rigorous student standards such as the Common Core State Standards (CCSS)/ College and Career Readiness Anchor (CCRA) Standards.

Step 2: Preparation and Questions

Users examine artifacts that the teacher provided as evidence of preparing the lesson. The planning artifacts in an Instructional Set will include the lesson plans and related artifacts such as student assignments, if appropriate. Examining the planning artifacts and jotting down what to look for will help prepare users for viewing the video of the classroom lesson. Users will also generate questions that they have about the artifacts and use those questions when discussing the lesson with their colleagues.

Step 3: Viewing the Classroom Video

Users view the video of the full lesson and note significant behaviors of the teacher and students. Some of the Instructional Sets include samples of student work. The samples were selected by the teacher and do not include teacher comments. If student work is included, users will review it after viewing the video.

Step 4: Selected Highlights of the Lesson Video

This step provides a summary of important teacher and student behaviors that happened in the lesson, and which aspects of the teaching and learning are being exemplified. These noteworthy behaviors will provide users with a lens for their examination of the lesson with their colleagues, and an opportunity to match the highlights with the FFT Clusters.

Step 5: Viewing the Teacher Commentary

Users watch the video of the teacher commentary about the lesson and the students, and jot down noteworthy information. A summary of the commentary and its relationship to effective aspects of teaching are provided.

Step 6: Questions, Applications, and Discussion

Prompts are provided that guide users in analyzing and reflecting on the Instructional Set. This step also includes a set of prompts for thinking about applications to a user's own practice.

Using the Study Guides

The power of professional learning comes when educators can have focused discussions about the teaching and learning that they witness. Individuals can use the Study Guides, but the process of discussing with colleagues what one has learned from the Instructional Set, and how it can be applied to one's own practice, is the action needed to enhance teaching and learning. Just watching videos of effective teachers is not enough to change practice. Additional thinking and actions are needed to effect change. Therefore, the Study Guides are intended for use by educators participating in professional learning communities.

The Guides can be used in any order, but it is recommended that users begin with a grade level and subject area with which they are comfortable.

There are two versions in each Study Guide: one for communities of teachers and one for communities of instructional coaches or mentors of teachers. The first five steps of the process are identical in both versions, and are designed to focus on examining the instruction. A group setting is not necessary for Steps 1–5. They can be completed at an individual's own pace.

Steps 1–5 could be completed as a whole group, though this is not recommended, since interaction is not part of these steps. Watching a 45-minute video is usually best done as an individual activity so the viewer can control the pacing and the volume or elect to wear headphones.

Step 6 requires participants to share their responses, observations, suggestions, and other insights. It is highly recommended that participants work in small groups, so all get an opportunity to contribute to the discussions. The facilitator could select highlights of the small group discussions to share with the whole group.

Step 6 is a group activity, focusing on analyses of the Instructional Set and applications of learning. The activities in Step

6 are similar in the two versions, but the discussions will be different in subtle ways because of the user's role.

Teachers	Instructional Coaches
Communities with all teachers will analyze and reflect on the Instructional Set in Step 6 and will identify an aspect of the learning that went well and another aspect that could be improved. Their colleagues in the community will discuss the analyses and suggest teaching techniques to support student learning as related to the featured lesson. After that activity, the teacher community will think about what they learned from the teacher and lesson, and how they might apply that learning to their own teaching.	*Communities with all coaches/mentors will analyze the Instructional Set in Step 6 and discuss how to prepare for a conversation with the featured teacher. Their colleagues in the community will discuss the analyses and planned questions, comments, and suggestions. Step 6 includes an activity that has the coaches thinking about what they learned from the teacher and lesson, and how they might apply it to their own coaching situation.*

There may be communities comprising educators with different roles, such as a combination of teachers, teacher leaders, and a mentor of beginning teachers. The prompts in Step 6 can be easily modified to accommodate their different roles. There also might be situations where the professional development is done in a whole group setting. Just as with the mixed group learning communities, the prompts and implementation can be modified to support the professional development of all participants.

The Study Guides should be treated as one possible way of using the Instructional Sets for professional growth among educational colleagues. The Guides do not advocate any particular model of coaching or professional learning. If practitioners have a certain model that is used in their district, then they should consider modifying Step 6 to meet their needs or requirements. Additional prompts or steps can be included to support their learning and accommodate their schedules.

Post-Study Activities

Learning communities are encouraged to use the Study Guides as a springboard for creating their own additional professional development activities.

The following example shows an additional set of prompts that could be completed after the learning community completes the activities in Step 6 of the Guide. It serves as a reflective activity and should be done by individuals, then shared with their colleagues.

Here's What, So What, Now What

    a. *Here's What:*   Identify five takeaways from your conversations with your colleagues. What examples did you collect?

    b. *So What:*   How do your takeaways connect to your current practice?

    c. *Now What:*   Based on the takeaways, identify 1–3 next steps you will take to inform your future practice.

Connection to the FFT Clusters

The Study Guides provide information and instructions on how to examine teaching and learning through the lens of the Framework for Teaching (FFT) Clusters. There are three versions of the FFT Clusters document: Generic, Literacy (ELA), and Mathematics. The Generic version reflects those instructional practices that are common across disciplines and was used for these Study Guides. The Literacy and Mathematics versions translate the general language of the narratives and critical attributes, where appropriate, into content-specific language.

Steps 1, 4, and 5 (lesson overview, lesson highlights, and teacher commentary) contain specific information about the Instructional Set and include prompts to match evidence to the related FFT Clusters. It is strongly suggested that copies of the FFT Clusters be available for participants so they can use them during their work with the Study Guides.

Even though the Guides were created with the FFT Clusters in mind, they also can be used to examine the Instructional Sets through the lens of the components of the Framework for Teaching. Practitioners who are familiar with the Framework for Teaching components will find the crosswalk between the Clusters and the components useful. It is located at the beginning of the FFT Clusters document. The FFT Clusters document can be downloaded for free individual use from the Danielson Group website: www.danielsongroup.org.

If practitioners use a different set of teaching standards than the Framework, they will still find the Study Guides and Instructional Sets useful for their professional growth needs. A crosswalk between their teaching standards and the FFT Clusters should be done so practitioners can associate the evidence in the Instructional Sets with their own standards.

Before you begin your examination of an Instructional Set's materials, you may want to check your equipment to make sure you can access the video and artifacts included with the Instructional Set. Enjoy studying the teaching and learning in the Instructional Set, and be prepared to enhance your own practice.

Looking at Teaching Through the Lens of the FFT Clusters

A Study Guide for
Teacher
Learning Communities

Teacher: Scurr
Subject: ELA
Grade: 4
Topic: Reading Workshop

Welcome to the Study Guide for the Jackson ELA Instructional Set, a collection of artifacts and videos for an instructional lesson. This Study Guide provides information and instructions on how to examine teaching and learning through the lens of the Framework for Teaching (FFT) Clusters. In order to complete the steps in this Guide, you will need access to the teacher's planning documents, the lesson video, and the teacher commentary video (http://www.danielsongroup.org/study-guides/). Steps 1–5 of this Study Guide focus on examining the Instructional Set and can be done by an individual. Step 6 is a group activity and focuses on sharing results of the analysis and applications of learning.

Step 1 - Lesson Overview

Read the background information of the lesson provided below.

This lesson consists of a whole-group discussion about a short story. The class is using the Jr. Great Books Program, and is to follow the protocol developed by that program for class discussions. The lesson is the fourth in a sequence, in which the students have read an American short story that can be found online, "Thank You, M'am," by Langston Hughes. The story features two characters, the young boy Roger, and an elderly woman, Mrs. Luella Bates Washington Jones. Hughes describes interactions that demonstrate transformation between the two characters. By explaining the story behind the crime and personalizing the characters, the author helps readers understand that Roger is not a bad kid as much as trapped in difficult circumstances. Hughes teaches through this story that everyone makes mistakes, but what is important is our individual decision to either learn from those mistakes or to continue making them. The story is used as the foundation for a sequence of several lessons. On the first day, the teacher read the story while the students followed along and asked questions about the story. On the second day, as the teacher read the story aloud again, the students focused on particular aspects of the text by making annotations on their copies in two different ways, indicating whether they thought someone was changing or not. They were to explain their thinking. On the third day, the students reviewed vocabulary.

In the story, the two characters meet when Roger attempts to steal Mrs. Jones's purse as she is walking home late at night. When Roger loses his balance, Mrs. Jones pulls him up and shakes him. She has Roger pick up her purse and begins scolding him, asking if he doesn't have someone at home to wash his face. After Roger answers no, Mrs. Jones tells him that it will get washed this evening and drags him up the street and into her house. After she has him wash his face, she feeds him and lectures him gently. Mrs. Jones tells him about her job at a hotel beauty shop, and shares that she herself has made many mistakes. Roger has a chance to run from Mrs. Jones's home, but he doesn't. Mrs. Jones gives him the money he was attempting to steal so that he can buy the blue suede shoes that he wants. As Roger is leaving, he wants to say something other than, "Thank you, ma'am" to Mrs. Jones. Although his lips moved, he couldn't even say that as he looked back at Mrs. Jones standing in the door. Mrs. Jones then shuts the door.

For the fourth day (the lesson in the video), the teacher has selected a focus question for the lesson. The question is: "Why does Mrs. Jones give Roger money for the blue suede shoes?"

Students are to write their first opinion about the question at the beginning of the lesson (this is not shown on the video). Interpreting events of a story is one of the central themes of the Literacy CCSS, making it an important element of any lesson that aims to prepare students to excel in those standards. It should be noted that the text does not explicitly state why Mrs. Jones gave Roger money for the blue suede shoes; students must support their ideas with evidence from the story, listen to one another, respond to each other directly, and be prepared to support their view with evidence from the text.

Step 2 - Preparation and Questions

- Read the teacher's lesson plan and jot down things you expect to see and what you want to look for in the video of the lesson.

- Write down any questions or comments you have about the lesson plan.

Step 3 – Viewing the Classroom Video

- View the complete video, noting those things you expected to see based on the lesson plan. Also note what was missing based on your expectations from the lesson plan. Jot down significant behaviors by the teacher and students pertinent to the FFT Clusters.

Step 4 – Selected Highlights of the Lesson Video

Read the highlights of the lesson provided below. Note those matching your highlights of the lesson. For each set of statements, determine the FFT Cluster that is best related to the behaviors presented.

The teacher demonstrates a depth of important content knowledge reflective of the standards for English Language Arts. The instructional planning document and interview reflect the teacher's knowledge of anchor and grade-level literacy standards, and the relationships between various sub-discipline literacy standards. The learning outcomes are aligned to the literacy standards. The instructional plan and the teacher commentary set this lesson up for a strong teaching performance. While the instructional purpose and learning tasks are thorough and clearly written in the planning document and explained in the interview, the lesson is not fully executed as described in those sources.

> A. The lesson plan includes two objectives, key vocabulary with definitions, connection to what students had read this week ("Thank You, M'am"), a lesson outline that includes Five Guidelines for Shared Inquiry discussion, a Focus Question, Cluster Questions, Closure, Differentiation, Assessment, and Day 5 Follow Up: Expository Writing: Explaining Evidence. (Cluster ___)

B. The teacher reviews Five Guidelines for Shared Inquiry with students at the beginning of the lesson. However, as the class discussion progresses, the teacher does not consistently model the guidelines. Students interrupt a current speaker at will without raising a hand, and the teacher sometimes turns and listens to the new speaker, without returning to the previous speaker. Once when this occurred, the student says, "Hey!" The teacher does not return to listen to this student; she continues listening to the student who interrupted. Occasionally, the teacher interrupts a student when they have just begun to speak, posing a new question. (Cluster ___)

C. The teacher and students do not consistently follow the discussion guidelines as explained by the teacher at the beginning of the lesson. The majority of the discussion is between teacher and individual students. (Cluster ___)

D. The teacher's facial expressions and tone of voice seem to indicate disagreement with a student's answer. (4:51–5:50) T: So you are asserting that the lesson she's trying to teach him is that he should buy shelter and other things and what evidence do you have for that? Student doesn't respond to the teacher. T: Is that what you were saying, yes or no? Student shakes head indicating no. The teacher immediately calls on another student. (Cluster ___)

E. The teacher reviews the Five Guidelines for Shared Inquiry before starting the discussion activity. She also uses the SmartBoard to display these guidelines. The Focus Question is displayed on a poster. (Cluster ___)

F. (53:20-54:40) While debriefing the "Our Collaboration" assessment, the teacher reads the phrases and has the students tell how they ranked the class as a whole. On the first statement, "Almost all of us contributed," a student says he thought only a few people did most of the talking. The teacher stopped the class and directs everyone who has said anything in class to raise their hand. She waits. She looks at students whose hands are not raised. She does not move on until every student has raised his or her hand. (Cluster ___)

G. Plans for smooth transitions (movement of the desks) are described in the lesson plan, but are not observed in the video. During the interview and in the lesson planning document, the teacher explains the arrangement of the seating in a square is for ease of viewing and discussion with classmates. Students are seated at desks arranged in a square that ensures visibility for the students of the teacher, the SmartBoard, and poster. (Cluster ___)

H. The classroom is a literacy-rich environment. Books are visible on shelves, grouped in containers, and many are labeled. One is labeled nonfiction. The books are placed at student level for easy access. Charts are posted on the wall. (Cluster ___)

I. When needed, to get students' attention, the teacher says, "Class?" The students, in unison respond, "Yes." (Cluster ___)

J. (46:00-47:00) Students become excited and loud at one point near the end of the lesson. One student stands up, talking loudly. The teacher uses a countdown 3-2-1, and says, "Class, classy, class." Students respond, "Yes!" and come to order. (Cluster ___)

K. The teacher tells students at the beginning of the lesson that they are to directly respond to one another's ideas. Few students directly make reference to another student's comments. Virtually all student comments are directed toward the teacher. (Cluster ___)

L. Activities are teacher-led. The discussion activity doesn't evolve into a discussion between students. (Cluster ___)

M. The teacher's lesson plan anticipates the shared discussion activity will take around 30 minutes. The activity lasts about 46 minutes (1:10–47:00). Students appear to grow restless as the lesson progresses, yawning, stretching, and not turning to the page of the text being shared. (Cluster ___)

N. The teacher monitors student learning by repeatedly asking the Focus question, "Why does Mrs. Jones give Roger money for the blue suede shoes?" She asks additional cluster questions she has listed in her lesson plan to extend students' learning during discussion and/or as follow-up questions. When the teacher asks the additional cluster questions, students continually respond to the original focus question. During the second half of the discussion, most students repeat a previously-given answer. (Cluster ___)

O. (47:00-50:00) After the shared discussion activity, the teacher directs students to amend, change, or retain their original answer to the Focus question on their Building Your Answer journal page. The teacher walks around, examining students' work and providing feedback to some students. Students have three minutes to complete the Building Answer Form. All students do not finish in this time period. (Cluster ___)

P. Of the five "Building Your Answer" student samples provided as artifacts, two students retain their original answer and three students changed/amended their answer. Four of the students support their answer by quoting text. One student supports the initial answer by quoting text. (Cluster ___)

Q. (56:00-57:34) The teacher tells the students to write down what they think their goal should be for the next time. She tells them she wants to know what they think about each of the areas and where there may be some improvement. The sample of one student's goal written on "Our Collaboration" states: "We sould [sic] keep up the place [sic] and make it more clearer like show it in a different way." This is taken directly as written on the survey. The word "place" is circled and "PACE" is written above it. (Cluster ___)

R. The teacher interview does not contain a reflection on the student learning that took place, or how to adapt the lesson to further promote student learning in the future. The teacher describes noticing how certain students are more comfortable and their level of participation increases when they are seated closer to her and each other. (Cluster ___)

Step 5 – Viewing the Teacher Commentary

Watch the video of the teacher's commentary about the lesson and jot down any questions or comments you have about the commentary. Read the highlights below and identify the related FFT Cluster.

A. The teacher explains the five-day plan of the Junior Great Books program. This lesson is day four. The teacher describes the procedure being followed in the lesson, and how it fits with the discussion protocols in the Junior Great Books program. The protocol is designed to enable students to explore text in depth, and to discuss both agreeing and conflicting interpretations of events in the story. The teacher explains the author of the story is Langston Hughes, and the piece exposes them to some language with which they are unfamiliar. This was discussed on a previous day. She also explains how the lesson meets the goals of the Common Core. (Cluster ___)

B. The teacher describes what she has done prior to this lesson. The commentary does not contain a reflection on student learning that took place or how to adapt the lesson to further promote student learning in the future. The teacher does share that by seating certain students closer to her and each other, the students are more comfortable and their level of participation increases due to the partnering. (Cluster ___)

Step 6 – Questions, Applications, and Discussion

The purpose of this step is to prompt your analysis and reflection of the Instructional Set and to have you think about applications to your own practice.

1. **Teaching and Learning Related to the FFT Clusters**

The purpose of the activity is to increase your understanding of the relationship between the highlights of the Instructional Set and the FFT Clusters. Your identification of an FFT Cluster for each of the highlights is compared to the Cluster identified by the master coders. The Answer Key is located at the end of the activities. You have options on how to complete the comparison. Determine what might work best for your group's learning. Options include, but are not limited to the following.

- Look at the first set of highlights. Take a poll of what each group member identified as the related FFT Cluster. If all members said the same FFT Cluster, have one or two members say why. Compare the group's response to the answer sheet. Repeat for the remainder of the highlights.

OR

- Have each member take one or two highlights. State the correct answer for each one, and a reason why the highlight demonstrates that FFT Cluster. The member will facilitate a discussion if others had different responses, with the goal of having all understand the justification of the correct answer.

OR

- Have members check their own responses to all the highlights. If there are any incorrect answers, then the member selects one highlight and leads a discussion with the group to learn why others think the highlight matches the correct FFT Cluster.

OR

- Determine your own process to check and discuss the match between highlights and the FFT Clusters.

2. **Analysis and Reflection of the Instructional Set**

The purpose of this activity is for you to analyze and reflect on what you saw and heard in the artifacts and videos, to share your analysis with your peers, and to discuss some of the questions or comments you noted. Review the notes, comments, and questions you recorded when you examined the Instructional Set.

- Identify a key teaching and learning attribute demonstrated in the Instructional Set that was effective and state why you think it worked well.

- Identify a different attribute and provide ideas about how it could be enhanced or improved.

- Share your statements with your group and have your peers react to and build upon your analysis and ideas.

Sample statements:

I noticed both in the instructional planning document and teacher commentary, Ms. Jackson demonstrates knowledge of anchor and grade-level literacy standards, and of the relationships between the standards of sub-disciplines of literacy. The lesson outline indicates the thoroughness of the pre-planning for the lesson by including the "Five Guidelines for Shared Inquiry" discussion, focus question, cluster questions, closure, differentiation, assessment, and the Day 5 Follow Up: "Expository Writing: Explaining Evidence."

The teacher reviewed the "Five Guidelines for Shared Inquiry" discussion with students at the beginning of the lesson:

1. Only those who have read the selection may take part in discussion.
2. Discussion is restricted to the selection that everyone has read.
3. Support for opinions should be found within the selection.
4. Listen to other participants, respond to them directly, and ask them questions.
5. Leaders may only ask questions—they may not answer them.

I noticed when the teacher paused as she explained each of the "Five Guidelines," most of the students filled in the word at the end of each guideline, indicating their understanding of the process. On reflection, I think the students were most successful with the first three guidelines, based on the students consistently following these guidelines. I think additional work needs to be done with guidelines 4 and 5, based on the inconsistency of the students following these two. The entire class would benefit from having more opportunities to practice the process of listening to other students, responding to them directly, and asking questions. Teacher consistency in requiring student leaders to only ask questions and not answer them would reinforce adherence to guideline 5.

Additional ideas for statements:

- Degree to which students take pride in their work and demonstrate a commitment to mastering challenging content

- Extent to which the instructional strategies used by the teacher are appropriate for the discipline

- Extent to which students monitor their own learning and provide feedback to others

- Extent to which the teacher provides wait time following questions, allowing students time to think and to construct an answer

6. **Notice, Learn, and Apply**

The purpose of this activity is for you to reflect on what you learned from your analysis of the Instructional Set and to determine how you will apply it to your teaching.

- Complete the statements:
  "I noticed _____."
  (Insert one thing you noticed about the teacher or students.)

  "And I learned _____."
  (State what you learned related to what you noticed.)

  "I will apply what I learned by _____."
  (Provide example of how you will use what you learned in your own context.)

- Share your statements with your group. Have others react and add how they might apply what you noticed to their own teaching context.

Sample statement:

- I noticed as the lesson progressed, it was not being fully executed as written in the planning document and explained in the commentary. I assumed the lesson and interactions with students would be smooth, engaging, and successful based on the thoroughness of the planning document. The teacher repeatedly clarified the learning task to assist students during the "Shared Inquiry" discussion. Students did not consistently cite text when answering the questions.

- I learned that thorough planning does not always ensure the lesson will go smoothly.

- I will apply what I learned by stopping when a lesson is not going as I planned, and addressing what is not working before moving forward.

Study Guide for Teachers Answer Key

Highlights from the Lesson Video (Step 4)

A. The lesson plan includes two objectives, key vocabulary with definitions, connection to what students had read this week ("Thank You, M'am"), a lesson outline that includes Five Guidelines for Shared Inquiry discussion, a Focus Question, Cluster Questions, Closure, Differentiation, Assessment, and Day 5 Follow Up: Expository Writing: Explaining Evidence. (Cluster 1 Clarity of Instructional Purpose and Accuracy of Content)

B. The teacher reviews Five Guidelines for Shared Inquiry discussion with students at the beginning of the lesson. However, as the class discussion progresses, the teacher does not consistently model the guidelines. Students interrupt a current speaker at will without raising a hand, and the teacher sometimes turns and listens to the new speaker, without returning to the previous speaker. Once when this occurred, the student says, "Hey!" The teacher does not return to listen to this student; she continues listening to the student who interrupted. Occasionally, the teacher interrupts a student when they have just begun to speak, posing a new question. (Cluster 1 Clarity of Instructional Purpose and Accuracy of Content)

C. The teacher and students do not consistently follow the discussion guidelines as explained by the teacher at the beginning of the lesson. The majority of the discussion is between teacher and individual students. (Cluster 2 Safe, Respectful, Supportive, and Challenging Learning Environment)

D. The teacher's facial expressions and tone of voice seem to indicate disagreement with a student's answer. (4:51–5:50) T: So you are asserting that the lesson she's trying to teach him is that he should buy shelter and other things and what evidence do you have for that? Student doesn't respond to the teacher. T: Is that what you were saying, yes or no? Student shakes head indicating no. The teacher immediately calls on another student. (Cluster 2 Safe, Respectful, Supportive, and Challenging Learning Environment)

E. The teacher reviews the Five Guidelines for Shared Inquiry before starting the discussion activity. She also uses the Smartboard to display these guidelines. The Focus Question is displayed on a poster. (Cluster 3 Classroom Management)

F. (53:20-54:40) While debriefing the "Our Collaboration" assessment, the teacher reads the phrases and has the students tell how they ranked the class as a whole. On the first statement, "Almost all of us contributed," a student says he thought only a few people did most of the talking. The teacher stopped the class and directs everyone who has said anything in class to raise their hand. She waits. She looks at students whose hands are not raised. She does not move on until every student has raised his or her hand. (Cluster 2 Safe, Respectful, Supportive, and Challenging Learning Environment)

Study Guide for Teachers Answer Key

Highlights from the Lesson Video (Step 4—cont'd.)

G. Plans for smooth transitions (movement of the desks) are described in the lesson plan, but are not observed in the video. During the interview and in the lesson planning document, the teacher explains the arrangement of the seating in a square is for ease of viewing and discussion with classmates. Students are seated at desks arranged in a square that ensures visibility for the students of the teacher, the SmartBoard, and poster. (Cluster 3 Classroom Management)

H. The classroom is a literacy-rich environment. Books are visible on shelves, grouped in containers, and many are labeled. One is labeled non-fiction. The books are placed at student level for easy access. Charts are posted on the wall. (Cluster 3 Classroom Management)

I. When needed, to get students' attention, the teacher says, "Class?" The students, in unison respond, "Yes." (Cluster 3 Classroom Management)

J. (46:00-47:00) Students become excited and loud at one point near the end of the lesson. One student stands up, talking loudly. The teacher uses a countdown 3- 2-1, and says, "Class, classy, class." Students respond, "Yes!" and come to order. (Cluster 3 Classroom Management)

K. The teacher tells students at the beginning of the lesson that they are to directly respond to one another's ideas. Few students directly make reference to another student's comments. Virtually all student comments are directed toward the teacher. (Cluster 4 Student Intellectual Engagement)

L. Activities are teacher-led. The discussion activity doesn't evolve into a discussion between students. (Cluster 4 Student Intellectual Engagement)

M. The teacher's lesson plan anticipates the shared discussion activity will take around 30 minutes. The activity lasts about 46 minutes (1:10–47:00). Students appear to grow restless as the lesson progresses, yawning, stretching, and not turning to the page of the text being shared. (Cluster 4 Student Intellectual Engagement)

N. The teacher monitors student learning by repeatedly asking the Focus question, "Why does Mrs. Jones give Roger money for the blue suede shoes?" She asks additional cluster questions she has listed in her lesson plan to extend students' learning during discussion and/or as follow-up questions. When the teacher asks the additional cluster questions, students continually respond to the original focus question. During the second half of the discussion, most students repeat a previously-given answer. (Cluster 5 Successful Learning by All Students)

O. (47:00-50:00) After the shared discussion activity, the teacher directs students to amend, change, or retain their original answer to the Focus question on their Building Your Answer journal page. The teacher walks around, examining students' work and providing feedback to some students. Students have three minutes to

Study Guide for Teachers Answer Key

Highlights from the Lesson Video (Step 4—cont'd.)

complete the Building Answer Form. All students do not finish in this time period. (Cluster 5 Successful Learning by All Students)

P. Of the five "Building Your Answer" student samples provided as artifacts, two students retain their original answer and three students changed/amended their answer. Four of the students support their answer by quoting text. One student supports the initial answer by quoting text. (Cluster 5 Successful Learning by All Students)

Q. (56:00-57:34) The teacher tells the students to write down what they think their goal should be for the next time. She tells them she wants to know what they think about each of the areas and where there may be some improvement. The sample of one student's goal written on "Our Collaboration" states: "We sould [sic] keep up the place [sic] and make it more clearer like show it in a different way. This is taken directly as written on the survey. The word "place" is circled and "PACE" is written above it. (Cluster 5 Successful Learning by All Students)

R. The teacher interview does not contain a reflection on the student learning that took place, or how to adapt the lesson to further promote student learning in the future. The teacher describes noticing how certain students are more comfortable and their level of participation increases when they are seated closer to her and each other. (Cluster 5 Successful Learning by All Students)

Study Guide for Teachers Answer Key

Highlights from the Teacher Commentary (Step 5)

A. The teacher explains the five-day plan of the Junior Great Books program. This lesson is day four. The teacher describes the procedure being followed in the lesson, and how it fits with the discussion protocols in the Junior Great Books program. The protocol is designed to enable students to explore text in depth, and to discuss both agreeing and conflicting interpretations of events in the story. The teacher explains the author of the story is Langston Hughes, and the piece exposes them to some language with which they are unfamiliar. This was discussed on a previous day. She also explains how the lesson meets the goals of Common Core. (Cluster 1 Clarity of Instructional Purpose and Accuracy of Content)

B. The teacher describes what she has done prior to this lesson. The commentary does not contain a reflection on student learning that took place or how to adapt the lesson to further promote student learning in the future. The teacher does share that by seating certain students closer to her and each other, the students are more comfortable and their level of participation increases due to the partnering. (Cluster 5 Successful Learning by All Students)

**Looking at Teaching Through
the Lens of the FFT Clusters**

A Study Guide for
Instructional Coach
Learning Communities

Teacher: Scurr
Subject: ELA
Grade: 4
Topic: Reading Workshop

Welcome to the Study Guide for the Jackson ELA Instructional Set, a collection of artifacts and videos for an instructional lesson. This Study Guide provides information and instructions on how to examine teaching and learning through the lens of the Framework for Teaching (FFT) Clusters. In order to complete the steps in this Guide, you will need access to the teacher's planning documents, the lesson video, and the teacher commentary video (http://www.danielsongroup.org/study-guides/). Steps 1–5 of this Study Guide focus on examining the Instructional Set and can be done by an individual. Step 6 is a group activity and focuses on sharing results of the analysis and applications of learning.

Step 1 - Lesson Overview

Read the background information of the lesson provided below.

This lesson consists of a whole-group discussion about a short story. The class is using the Jr. Great Books Program, and is to follow the protocol developed by that program for class discussions. The lesson is the fourth in a sequence, in which the students have read an American short story that can be found online, "Thank You, M'am," by Langston Hughes. The story features two characters, the young boy Roger, and an elderly woman, Mrs. Luella Bates Washington Jones. Hughes describes interactions that demonstrate transformation between the two characters. By explaining the story behind the crime and personalizing the characters, the author helps readers understand that Roger is not a bad kid as much as trapped in difficult circumstances. Hughes teaches through this story that everyone makes mistakes, but what is important is our individual decision to either learn from those mistakes or to continue making them. The story is used as the foundation for a sequence of several lessons. On the first day, the teacher read the story while the students followed along and asked questions about the story. On the second day, as the teacher read the story aloud again, the students focused on particular aspects of the text by making annotations on their copies in two different ways, indicating whether they thought someone was changing or not. They were to explain their thinking. On the third day, the students reviewed vocabulary.

In the story, the two characters meet when Roger attempts to steal Mrs. Jones's purse as she is walking home late at night. When Roger loses his balance, Mrs. Jones pulls him up and shakes him. She has Roger pick up her purse and begins scolding him, asking if he doesn't have someone at home to wash his face. After Roger answers no, Mrs. Jones tells him that it will get washed this evening and drags him up the street and into her house. After she has him wash his face, she feeds him and lectures him gently. Mrs. Jones tells him about her job at a hotel beauty shop, and shares that she herself has made many mistakes. Roger has a chance to run from Mrs. Jones's home, but he doesn't. Mrs. Jones gives him the money he was attempting to steal so that he can buy the blue suede shoes that he wants. As Roger is leaving, he wants to say something other than, "Thank you, ma'am" to Mrs. Jones. Although his lips moved, he couldn't even say that as he looked back at Mrs. Jones standing in the door. Mrs. Jones then shuts the door.

For the fourth day (the lesson in the video), the teacher has selected a focus question for the lesson. The question is: "Why does Mrs. Jones give Roger money for the blue suede shoes?" Students are to write their first opinion about the question at the beginning of the lesson (this is not shown on the video). Interpreting events of a story is one of the central themes of the Literacy CCSS, making it an important element of any lesson that aims to prepare students to excel in those standards. It should be noted that the text does not explicitly state why Mrs. Jones gave Roger money for the blue suede shoes; students must support their ideas with evidence from the story, listen to one another, respond to each other directly, and be prepared to support their view with evidence from the text.

Step 2 - Preparation and Questions

- *Read the teacher's lesson plan and jot down things you expect to see and what you want to look for in the video of the lesson.*

- *Write down any questions or comments you have about the lesson plan.*

Step 3 – Viewing the Classroom Video

- *View the complete video, noting those things you expected to see based on the lesson plan. Also note what was missing based on your expectations from the lesson plan. Jot down significant behaviors by the teacher and students pertinent to the FFT Clusters.*

Step 4 – Selected Highlights of the Lesson Video

Read the highlights of the lesson provided below. Note those matching your highlights of the lesson. For each set of statements, determine the FFT Cluster that is best related to the behaviors presented.

The teacher demonstrates a depth of important content knowledge reflective of the standards for English Language Arts. The instructional planning document and interview reflect the teacher's knowledge of anchor and grade-level literacy standards, and the relationships between various sub-discipline literacy standards. The learning outcomes are aligned to the literacy standards. The instructional plan and the teacher commentary set this lesson up for a strong teaching performance. While the instructional purpose and learning tasks are thorough and clearly written in the planning document and explained in the interview, the lesson is not fully executed as described in those sources.

> A. The lesson plan includes two objectives, key vocabulary with definitions, connection to what students had read this week ("Thank You, M'am"), a lesson outline that includes Five Guidelines for Shared Inquiry discussion, a Focus Question, Cluster Questions, Closure, Differentiation, Assessment, and Day 5 Follow Up: Expository Writing: Explaining Evidence. (Cluster ___)

B. The teacher reviews Five Guidelines for Shared Inquiry with students at the beginning of the lesson. However, as the class discussion progresses, the teacher does not consistently model the guidelines. Students interrupt a current speaker at will without raising a hand, and the teacher sometimes turns and listens to the new speaker, without returning to the previous speaker. Once when this occurred, the student says, "Hey!" The teacher does not return to listen to this student; she continues listening to the student who interrupted. Occasionally, the teacher interrupts a student when they have just begun to speak, posing a new question. (Cluster ___)

C. The teacher and students do not consistently follow the discussion guidelines as explained by the teacher at the beginning of the lesson. The majority of the discussion is between teacher and individual students. (Cluster ___)

D. The teacher's facial expressions and tone of voice seem to indicate disagreement with a student's answer. (4:51–5:50) T: So you are asserting that the lesson she's trying to teach him is that he should buy shelter and other things and what evidence do you have for that? Student doesn't respond to the teacher. T: Is that what you were saying, yes or no? Student shakes head indicating no. The teacher immediately calls on another student. (Cluster ___)

E. The teacher reviews the Five Guidelines for Shared Inquiry before starting the discussion activity. She also uses the SmartBoard to display these guidelines. The Focus Question is displayed on a poster. (Cluster ___)

F. (53:20-54:40) While debriefing the "Our Collaboration" assessment, the teacher reads the phrases and has the students tell how they ranked the class as a whole. On the first statement, "Almost all of us contributed," a student says he thought only a few people did most of the talking. The teacher stopped the class and directs everyone who has said anything in class to raise their hand. She waits. She looks at students whose hands are not raised. She does not move on until every student has raised his or her hand. (Cluster ___)

G. Plans for smooth transitions (movement of the desks) are described in the lesson plan, but are not observed in the video. During the interview and in the lesson planning document, the teacher explains the arrangement of the seating in a square is for ease of viewing and discussion with classmates. Students are seated at desks arranged in a square that ensures visibility for the students of the teacher, the SmartBoard, and poster. (Cluster ___)

H. The classroom is a literacy-rich environment. Books are visible on shelves, grouped in containers, and many are labeled. One is labeled nonfiction. The books are placed at student level for easy access. Charts are posted on the wall. (Cluster ___)

I. When needed, to get students' attention, the teacher says, "Class?" The students, in unison respond, "Yes." (Cluster ___)

J. (46:00-47:00) Students become excited and loud at one point near the end of the lesson. One student stands up, talking loudly. The teacher uses a countdown 3-2-1, and says, "Class, classy, class." Students respond, "Yes!" and come to order. (Cluster ___)

K. The teacher tells students at the beginning of the lesson that they are to directly respond to one another's ideas. Few students directly make reference to another student's comments. Virtually all student comments are directed toward the teacher. (Cluster ___)

L. Activities are teacher-led. The discussion activity doesn't evolve into a discussion between students. (Cluster ___)

M. The teacher's lesson plan anticipates the shared discussion activity will take around 30 minutes. The activity lasts about 46 minutes (1:10–47:00). Students appear to grow restless as the lesson progresses, yawning, stretching, and not turning to the page of the text being shared. (Cluster ___)

N. The teacher monitors student learning by repeatedly asking the Focus question, "Why does Mrs. Jones give Roger money for the blue suede shoes?" She asks additional cluster questions she has listed in her lesson plan to extend students' learning during discussion and/or as follow-up questions. When the teacher asks the additional cluster questions, students continually respond to the original focus question. During the second half of the discussion, most students repeat a previously-given answer. (Cluster ___)

O. (47:00-50:00) After the shared discussion activity, the teacher directs students to amend, change, or retain their original answer to the Focus question on their Building Your Answer journal page. The teacher walks around, examining students' work and providing feedback to some students. Students have three minutes to complete the Building Answer Form. All students do not finish in this time period. (Cluster ___)

P. Of the five "Building Your Answer" student samples provided as artifacts, two students retain their original answer and three students changed/amended their answer. Four of the students support their answer by quoting text. One student supports the initial answer by quoting text. (Cluster ___)

Q. (56:00-57:34) The teacher tells the students to write down what they think their goal should be for the next time. She tells them she wants to know what they think about each of the areas and where there may be some improvement. The sample of one student's goal written on "Our Collaboration" states: "We sould [sic] keep up the place [sic] and make it more clearer like show it in a different way." This is taken directly as written on the survey. The word "place" is circled and "PACE" is written above it. (Cluster ___)

R. The teacher interview does not contain a reflection on the student learning that took place, or how to adapt the lesson to further promote student learning in the future. The teacher describes noticing how certain students are more comfortable and their level of participation increases when they are seated closer to her and each other. (Cluster ___)

Step 5 – Viewing the Teacher Commentary

Watch the video of the teacher's commentary about the lesson and jot down any questions or comments you have about the commentary. Read the highlights below and identify the related FFT Cluster.

A. The teacher explains the five-day plan of the Junior Great Books program. This lesson is day four. The teacher describes the procedure being followed in the lesson, and how it fits with the discussion protocols in the Junior Great Books program. The protocol is designed to enable students to explore text in depth, and to discuss both agreeing and conflicting interpretations of events in the story. The teacher explains the author of the story is Langston Hughes, and the piece exposes them to some language with which they are unfamiliar. This was discussed on a previous day. She also explains how the lesson meets the goals of the Common Core. (Cluster ___)

B. The teacher describes what she has done prior to this lesson. The commentary does not contain a reflection on student learning that took place or how to adapt the lesson to further promote student learning in the future. The teacher does share that by seating certain students closer to her and each other, the students are more comfortable and their level of participation increases due to the partnering. (Cluster ___)

Step 6 – Questions, Applications, and Discussion

The purpose of this step is to prompt your analysis and reflection of the Instructional Set and to have you think about applications to your own practice.

1. **Teaching and Learning Related to the FFT Clusters**

    The purpose of the activity is to increase your understanding of the relationship between the highlights of the Instructional Set and the FFT Clusters. Your identification of an FFT Cluster for each of the highlights is compared to the Cluster identified by the master coders. The Answer Key is located at the end of the activities. You have options on how to complete the comparison. Determine what might work best for your group's learning. Options include, but are not limited to the following.

    - Look at the first set of highlights. Take a poll of what each group member identified as the related FFT Cluster. If all members said the same FFT Cluster, then have one or two members say why. Compare the group's response to the answer sheet. Repeat for the remainder of the sets of highlights.

    OR

    - Have each member take one or two sets of highlights and be the discussant for them. The discussant will state the correct answer and state a reason why the statements in the set demonstrate the FFT Cluster. The discussant will facilitate a discussion if members had different responses with the goal of all understanding the justification of the correct answer.

    OR

- Have members check their own responses to all the sets of highlights. If there are any incorrect answers, then the member selects one set and leads a discussion with the group to learn why others think the highlights match the correct FFT Cluster.

OR

- Determine your own process to check and discuss the match between highlights and the FFT Clusters.

2. **Analysis and Reflection of the Instructional Set**

The purpose of this activity is for you to analyze and reflect on what you saw and heard in the artifacts and videos and to discuss some of the questions or comments you noted. One element of a professional conversation is asking questions to ascertain more information about a teacher's thinking and the behaviors of both students and teacher. This activity allows you and your peers to practice preparing such questions. Your peers can comment on whether your questions are appropriate and will obtain useful information without making the featured teacher feel uneasy or criticized.

The second part of this activity focuses on helping teachers move their practice forward. Please note that having you prepare for and model an entire conversation about the lesson with the featured teacher is not the purpose of this activity as written. Your group can modify or replace the activity to meet your group's needs

- Review the notes, comments, and questions you recorded when you examined the Instructional Set. Pretend you have the opportunity to ask the teacher some questions to get additional information about the strategies used or decisions made for this Instructional Set.

- Share with your group just the questions you would use with the teacher to elicit additional information. Have your peers comment about your questions and add other questions they had about the same event.

- Share with others in your group what you would do to prompt the teacher's thinking and actions to enhance his/her practice. Take turns sharing and discussing the prompts.

Sample A, Part I:

In debriefing the "Our Collaboration" survey assessment, you had students tell how they ranked the class a whole. After you read the first statement, "Almost all of us contribute," a student says he thought only a few people did most of the talking. In response to his answer, you directed everyone who has said anything in class to raise their hands. Can you recall your thoughts when you polled the class and addressed the student about his answer?

Sample A, Part II:

What other strategies have you tried when either that student's or other students' answers are not correct or not the answer you are seeking? Might any of those strategies have worked in this situation? Are there some other techniques that might work with the students in this class?

Sample B, Part I:

In the lesson plan, you anticipate it will take around 30 minutes to do the shared discussion activity. The shared discussion activity lasts about 46 minutes (1:10–47:00). Students began to grow restless as the lesson progressed, yawning, stretching, and not turning to the page of the text being cited. Why might that activity have taken longer than you initially planned?

Sample B, Part II:

If you had the opportunity to teach this lesson again, what are some things you would consider changing to help the students stay engaged and on task during the shared discussion activity? When might you have transitioned from the shared discussion activity to the next activity? Why at that time? Will there be lessons in the near future where you can try doing this?

3. **Notice, Learn, and Apply**

The purpose of this activity is for you to reflect on what you learned from your analysis of the Instructional Set and to determine how you will apply it to your teaching.

- Complete the statements:
  "I noticed _____."
  (Insert one thing you noticed about the teacher or students.)

  "And I learned _____."
  (State what you learned related to what you noticed.)

  "I will apply what I learned by _____."
  (Provide example of how you will use what you learned in your own context.)

- Share your statements with your group. Have others react and add how they might apply what you noticed to their own coaching context.

Sample statements:

- I noticed that at times during the lesson, it appeared that the teacher's facial expressions, comments, and tone of voice reflected negatively in her interactions with some students. This could contribute to a perception that the environment is not always safe for risk-taking by all students.

- I learned that this is difficult for me to address with the teacher because it is personal as well as professional.

- I will apply what I have learned by planning to use appropriate coaching skills at all times to address individual personal situations before conferencing with the teacher. If needed, I will also seek advice from others and research coaching skills to address the situation.

Study Guide for Instructional Coaches Answer Key
Highlights from the Lesson Video (Step 4)

A. The lesson plan includes two objectives, key vocabulary with definitions, connection to what students had read this week ("Thank You, M'am"), a lesson outline that includes Five Guidelines for Shared Inquiry discussion, a Focus Question, Cluster Questions, Closure, Differentiation, Assessment, and Day 5 Follow Up: Expository Writing: Explaining Evidence. (Cluster 1 Clarity of Instructional Purpose and Accuracy of Content)

B. The teacher reviews Five Guidelines for Shared Inquiry discussion with students at the beginning of the lesson. However, as the class discussion progresses, the teacher does not consistently model the guidelines. Students interrupt a current speaker at will without raising a hand, and the teacher sometimes turns and listens to the new speaker, without returning to the previous speaker. Once when this occurred, the student says, "Hey!" The teacher does not return to listen to this student; she continues listening to the student who interrupted. Occasionally, the teacher interrupts a student when they have just begun to speak, posing a new question. (Cluster 1 Clarity of Instructional Purpose and Accuracy of Content)

C. The teacher and students do not consistently follow the discussion guidelines as explained by the teacher at the beginning of the lesson. The majority of the discussion is between teacher and individual students. (Cluster 2 Safe, Respectful, Supportive, and Challenging Learning Environment)

D. The teacher's facial expressions and tone of voice seem to indicate disagreement with a student's answer. (4:51–5:50) T: So you are asserting that the lesson she's trying to teach him is that he should buy shelter and other things and what evidence do you have for that? Student doesn't respond to the teacher. T: Is that what you were saying, yes or no? Student shakes head indicating no. The teacher immediately calls on another student. (Cluster 2 Safe, Respectful, Supportive, and Challenging Learning Environment)

E. The teacher reviews the Five Guidelines for Shared Inquiry before starting the discussion activity. She also uses the Smartboard to display these guidelines. The Focus Question is displayed on a poster. (Cluster 3 Classroom Management)

F. (53:20-54:40) While debriefing the "Our Collaboration" assessment, the teacher reads the phrases and has the students tell how they ranked the class as a whole. On the first statement, "Almost all of us contributed," a student says he thought only a few people did most of the talking. The teacher stopped the class and directs everyone who has said anything in class to raise their hand. She waits. She looks at students whose hands are not raised. She does not move on until every student has raised his or her hand. (Cluster 2 Safe, Respectful, Supportive, and Challenging Learning Environment)

Study Guide for Instructional Coaches Answer Key
Highlights from the Lesson Video (Step 4—cont'd.)

G. Plans for smooth transitions (movement of the desks) are described in the lesson plan, but are not observed in the video. During the interview and in the lesson planning document, the teacher explains the arrangement of the seating in a square is for ease of viewing and discussion with classmates. Students are seated at desks arranged in a square that ensures visibility for the students of the teacher, the SmartBoard, and poster. (Cluster 3 Classroom Management)

H. The classroom is a literacy-rich environment. Books are visible on shelves, grouped in containers, and many are labeled. One is labeled nonfiction. The books are placed at student level for easy access. Charts are posted on the wall. (Cluster 3 Classroom Management)

I. When needed, to get students' attention, the teacher says, "Class?" The students, in unison respond, "Yes." (Cluster 3 Classroom Management)

J. (46:00-47:00) Students become excited and loud at one point near the end of the lesson. One student stands up, talking loudly. The teacher uses a countdown 3- 2-1, and says, "Class, classy, class." Students respond, "Yes!" and come to order. (Cluster 3 Classroom Management)

K. The teacher tells students at the beginning of the lesson that they are to directly respond to one another's ideas. Few students directly make reference to another student's comments. Virtually all student comments are directed toward the teacher. (Cluster 4 Student Intellectual Engagement)

L. Activities are teacher-led. The discussion activity doesn't evolve into a discussion between students. (Cluster 4 Student Intellectual Engagement)

M. The teacher's lesson plan anticipates the shared discussion activity will take around 30 minutes. The activity lasts about 46 minutes (1:10–47:00). Students appear to grow restless as the lesson progresses, yawning, stretching, and not turning to the page of the text being shared. (Cluster 4 Student Intellectual Engagement)

N. The teacher monitors student learning by repeatedly asking the Focus question, "Why does Mrs. Jones give Roger money for the blue suede shoes?" She asks additional cluster questions she has listed in her lesson plan to extend students' learning during discussion and/or as follow-up questions. When the teacher asks the additional cluster questions, students continually respond to the original focus question. During the second half of the discussion, most students repeat a previously-given answer. (Cluster 5 Successful Learning by All Students)

O. (47:00-50:00) After the shared discussion activity, the teacher directs students to amend, change, or retain their original answer to the Focus question on their Building Your Answer journal page. The teacher walks around, examining students' work and providing feedback to some students. Students have three minutes to complete the Building Answer Form. All

Study Guide for Instructional Coaches Answer Key
Highlights from the Lesson Video (Step 4—cont'd.)

students do not finish in this time period. (Cluster 5 Successful Learning by All Students)

P. Of the five "Building Your Answer" student samples provided as artifacts, two students retain their original answer and three students changed/amended their answer. Four of the students support their answer by quoting text. One student supports the initial answer by quoting text. (Cluster 5 Successful Learning by All Students)

Q. (56:00-57:34) The teacher tells the students to write down what they think their goal should be for the next time. She tells them she wants to know what they think about each of the areas and where there may be some improvement. The sample of one student's goal written on "Our Collaboration" states: "We sould [sic] keep up the place [sic] and make it more clearer like show it in a different way. This is taken directly as written on the survey. The word "place" is circled and "PACE" is written above it. (Cluster 5 Successful Learning by All Students)

R. The teacher interview does not contain a reflection on the student learning that took place, or how to adapt the lesson to further promote student learning in the future. The teacher describes noticing how certain students are more comfortable and their level of participation increases when they are seated closer to her and each other. (Cluster 5 Successful Learning by All Students)

Study Guide for Instructional Coaches Answer Key
Highlights from the Teacher Commentary (Step 5)

A. The teacher explains the five-day plan of the Junior Great Books program. This lesson is day four. The teacher describes the procedure being followed in the lesson, and how it fits with the discussion protocols in the Junior Great Books program. The protocol is designed to enable students to explore text in depth, and to discuss both agreeing and conflicting interpretations of events in the story. The teacher explains the author of the story is Langston Hughes, and the piece exposes them to some language with which they are unfamiliar. This was discussed on a previous day. She also explains how the lesson meets the goals of Common Core. (Cluster 1 Clarity of Instructional Purpose and Accuracy of Content)

B. The teacher describes what she has done prior to this lesson. The commentary does not contain a reflection on student learning that took place or how to adapt the lesson to further promote student learning in the future. The teacher does share that by seating certain students closer to her and each other, the students are more comfortable and their level of participation increases due to the partnering. (Cluster 5 Successful Learning by All Students)

Record of Evidence

This Record of Evidence (ROE) contains key evidence aligned to the FFT Clusters. Interpretive statements about the evidence are also provided. The ROE was created by two master coders who recorded evidence and interpretation statements independently, reviewed each others' work, and arrived at a final composite version based on their professional conversations. This version was reviewed by a leader of the master coders. The ROE is included in this Study Guide so users can see what master coders identified as key evidence, and their interpretation of that evidence through the lens of the FFT Clusters. It is provided as an example of one type of analysis of an Instructional Set. The ROEs were created for professional development rather than evaluative purposes. Users are cautioned about using them for teacher evaluation.

Rubric:	Generic
Grade:	4
Subject:	ELA
Topic:	Reading Workshop
Teacher description:	Female, African American
Class description:	19-21 students
Artifacts:	<ul><li>Lesson plan</li><li>Samples of student work (*Building Your Answer* and *Collaborative Assessment* form)</li><li>Teacher commentary</li></ul>
Length of video:	57:47

Record of Evidence

Cluster 1:   Clarity of Instructional Purpose and Accuracy of Content
Guiding Questions

- *To what extent does the teacher demonstrate depth of important content knowledge and conduct the class with a clear and ambitious purpose, reflective of the standards for the discipline and appropriate to the students' levels of knowledge and skill?*

- *To what degree are the elements of a lesson (the sequence of topics, instructional strategies, and materials and resources) well designed and executed, and aligned with the purpose of the lesson?*

- *To what extent are they designed to engage students in high-level learning in the discipline?*

Evidence

Instructional Plan
- The lesson plan lists and describes six Common Core State Standards (CCSS). Students will read the Langston Hughes story "Thank You M'am" to find textual evidence to answer the focus question, "Why does Mrs. Jones give Roger money for the blue suede shoes?" The lesson plan includes:
  - Two objectives
  - Key vocabulary with definitions
  - Connection to what students had read this week
  - "Thank You M'am" lesson outline
  - Five Guidelines for Shared Inquiry discussion
  - Focus Question
  - Cluster Questions
  - Closure
  - Differentiation
  - Assessment
  - Day 5 Expository Writing Follow Up: Explaining Evidence. Time allotted for review of the story writing questions: 10 minutes; for discussion: 30 minutes.
- Differentiation described in the lesson plan:
  - Display discussion guidelines and Focus Question
  - Extend time to compose a response and search for evidence to the interpretive question before discussion
  - Reconfigure seating in square for ease of viewing and discussion with classmates
  - Differentiate follow-up questions by idea, evidence, or response based on areas of difficulty or proficiency evidenced by students during the discussion.

Record of Evidence

Cluster 1: Clarity of Instructional Purpose and Accuracy of Content

Evidence (cont'd.)

- Other than the use of the Cluster Questions, the teacher does not address anticipated misconceptions and how she might monitor or clarify those misconceptions with the students.
- The follow-up lesson for the next day (expository writing) is included in the lesson plan to show progression and connections to the work.

Artifacts
- Student Samples:
    - *Building Your Answer* page of Reader's Journal
    - *Our Collaboration Assessment* form

Teacher Commentary
- The teacher explains the five-day plan of the Junior Great Books program. This lesson is day four when an interpretive question is discussed. The question was not posed on a previous day. Students are to write their first opinion about the question at the beginning of this lesson (this is not shown on the video). The teacher explains that the author of the story is Langston Hughes, and the piece exposes them to some language with which they unfamiliar. This was discussed on a previous day. She also explains how the lesson meets the goals of the Common Core. Although this text is fiction, the students also read non-fiction books based on another program the school uses. The teacher said she carefully selected the seating arrangement of the students for this discussion. She seated students next to peers with whom they were comfortable to encourage their participation in the discussion.

Video
- The teacher reviews with students the Five Guidelines for Shared Inquiry discussion at the beginning of the lesson. She pauses as she states each guideline, and students orally fill in the word at the end of the guideline statements.
- What is the title of the story? (Students answer her orally in unison).
- Listen to one another and speak to one another. I won't be answering your questions. I'm only posing questions.
- Use textual evidence to support your answers. Find your answers within the story. Give us the page number and read the part that supports your opinion.
- She tells students they have already read the story "Thank You M'am" twice. The teacher stresses that students must support their ideas with evidence from the story, listen to one another, and respond to each other directly. She further explains this means they are to talk to each other. She tells them that most importantly, they must not expect her to do anything but ask questions.

Record of Evidence

Cluster 1: Clarity of Instructional Purpose and Accuracy of Content

Evidence (cont'd.)

- T (as she explains the process for speaking to each other): Am I going to be offering my opinion?
- Ss: No.
- T: To be honest, I am not 100% certain as to the answer to the question either. So, okay, I'm looking for answers from you, so to repeat the focus question and to begin, why does Mrs. Jones give Roger the money for the blue suede shoes?
- The teacher does not consistently model the Five Guidelines for Shared Inquiry discussion as the class discussion progresses. Students interrupt a current speaker at will without raising a hand. The teacher sometimes turns and listens to the interrupting speaker without letting the original speaker finish. Once when this occurs, the original speaker says, "Hey!" The teacher does not return to listen to this student; she continues listening to the student who interrupted. Occasionally, the teacher interrupts a student when they have just begun to speak, posing a new question.
- Students do not consistently cite text when answering the Focus question.
- The shared discussion is mostly between the teacher and individual students. Minimum student-to-student discussion is observed.
- The teacher repeats the Focus question many times throughout the shared discussion, and occasionally reminds students of the process of speaking directly to each other.

Record of Evidence

Cluster 1:   Clarity of Instructional Purpose and Accuracy of Content

Interpretation

- The lesson plan is thorough in its content.

- No content errors are noted in the plan. It is aligned with grade level objectives and the CCSS.

- The lesson plan provides objectives and activities for reading, writing, and speaking.

- The teacher seems to have appropriate content knowledge and pedagogical skills for this class.

- The teacher describes in the interview how the Junior Great Books program provides opportunities for reading, writing, and discussion every week.

- Most students do not engage fully in the discussion using the Five Guidelines for Shared Inquiry as explained by the teacher. This indicates most students may not fully understand what they are to do.

- The teacher intermittently reminds students to give their peers wait time when some students have difficulty finding textual evidence. This strategy is not used with all students experiencing difficulty finding textual evidence.

Record of Evidence

Cluster 2: Safe, Respectful, Supportive, and Challenging Learning Environment

Guiding Questions

- *To what extent do the interactions between teacher and students, and among students, demonstrate genuine caring and a safe, respectful, supportive, and also challenging learning environment?*

- *Do teachers convey high expectations for student learning and encourage hard work and perseverance? Is the environment safe for risk taking?*

- *Do students take pride in their work and demonstrate a commitment to mastering challenging content?*

Evidence

- Students are to reflect on the focus question provided: "Why does Mrs. Jones give Roger money for the blue suede shoes?" The students become quiet when the teacher begins talking.

- The teacher and students do not consistently follow the discussion guidelines as explained by the teacher at the beginning of the lesson. The majority of the discussion is between teacher and individual students.

- Students occasionally use classmates' names when referring to each other. ("I agree with Shania and Joseph, because Roger tried to take Mrs. Jones's purse to get money to buy new shoes.")

- S (whispering to the girl sitting next to him): Where is it? She tells him. S: I want Joleah to read it. Joleah immediately begins to read the text.

- T (when a student coughs): I'm sorry, are you okay?

- Teacher's familiarity with individual student's interest or personality is minimally evident.

- T: I haven't heard from Kevin. Kevin would you like to join us?

- The teacher calls on students by name (Joseph, Laneice, Joleah, Shania, Ambre').

- The teacher sometimes uses humor with the students; e.g., when a student says "devilish ways," the teacher laughs and asks the student to explain.

- When students interrupt another student, or don't wait on a student to answer, the teacher occasionally says, "Give him/her a moment/minute."

- Some students begin to over talk one another as the discussion progresses, without holding up hands to indicate they have something to share. The teacher influences the conversation by looking toward someone even if that person interrupts the student who is speaking. Sometimes the teacher interrupts a student while they are speaking, interjecting a new question. This occurs a couple of times as students

Record of Evidence

Cluster 2: Safe, Respectful, Supportive, and Challenging Learning Environment

Evidence (cont'd.)

are just beginning to speak, at other times when students are in the midst of an explanation. The teacher uses volume to control the direction of a conversation. As her volume increases, so does the volume of the students. It sometimes becomes difficult to hear individual student answers.

- The teacher's facial expressions and tone of voice seem to imply that the teacher disagrees with the student's answer. (4:51–5:50) T: So you are asserting that the lesson she's trying to teach him is that he should buy shelter and other things and what evidence do you have for that? Student doesn't respond to the teacher. T: Is that what you were saying, yes or no? Student shakes head indicating no. The teacher immediately calls on another student.

- (53:20-54:40) In debriefing the Our Collaboration assessment, the teacher reads the phrases and has the students tell how they ranked the class as a whole. On the first statement, "Almost all of us contributed," a student says he thought only a few people did most of the talking. The teacher stops the class and directs everyone who has said anything in class to raise their hand. She waits until everyone has raised their hand. The teacher's facial expression, tone of voice, and comments seem to indicate she is attempting to challenge or sway the student about his response.

Record of Evidence

Cluster 2: Safe, Respectful, Supportive, and Challenging Learning Environment

Interpretation

- The discussion begins as soon as the teacher posts the focus questions and the guidelines for the discussion.
- The teacher's expectation for student learning varies. Some students give answers and the teacher encourages them to find and cite examples. This is not done with all students.
- Talk and interactions among students are mostly respectful.
- Students are respectful to the teacher.
- The teacher intermittently encourages a few students to speak who have not previously spoken.
- The teacher calls on some students to participate more than others.
- There are times when the teacher's words, facial expressions, tone, and comments do not consistently promote a safe environment conducive to student risk-taking.

Record of Evidence

Cluster 3: Classroom Management
Guiding Questions

- *Is the classroom well run and organized?*

- *Are classroom routines and procedures clear and carried out efficiently by both teacher and students with little loss of instructional time?*

- *To what extent do students themselves take an active role in their smooth operation?*

- *Are directions for activities clearly explained so that there is no confusion?*

- *Do students not only understand and comply with standards of conduct, but also play an active part in setting the tone for maintaining those standards?*

- *How does the physical environment support the learning activities?*

Evidence
- Papers and materials have been distributed to students before the video begins.
- Plans for smooth transitions (movement of the desks) are described in the lesson plan, but are not observed in the video. The teacher explains during the interview and in the planning document the arrangement of the seating in a square for ease of viewing and discussion with classmates. Students are seated at desks arranged in a square that allows visibility for the students of the teacher, each other, the SmartBoard, and poster.
- Books are placed at student level so the students can easily access them.
- The teacher says, "Class?" when needed to get students' attention The students respond in unison, "Yes."
- (46:00-47:00) There is a time near the end of the lesson when students are excited and become loud. One student stands up, talking loudly. The teacher uses a countdown 3- 2-1, and says, "Class, classy, class." Students chime, "Yes!" The students come to order.
- There is a teacher-made chart that describes Cooling Down Strategies for the students to use when needed.
- T (near the end of the lesson): I'll know you're finished when your books are closed and your pencils are down. Students comply with the teacher's directions immediately before the video ends.
- The teacher reviews the Five Guidelines for Shared Inquiry before starting the discussion activity. She also uses the SmartBoard to display these guidelines. The Focus Question is displayed on a poster.
- Most students raise hands to answer or ask a question before they speak. A few times students speak out without raising their hands, interrupting the student speaking.
- When the student sitting to the teacher's right is looking in his desk, the teacher continues speaking without pausing and gently touches him on his arm.

Record of Evidence

Cluster 3: Classroom Management

Evidence (cont'd.)

- Humming is heard several times during the lesson. The teacher doesn't address the humming. It doesn't appear to be noticed by others.
- Students show no reaction when the bell rings.
- The shared discussion activity lasts about 46 minutes. As the activity progresses, students appear to grow more restless, wiggling, laying heads on table, fiddling in desk, turning around, stretching, and yawning. This does not disrupt the learning environment as a whole.
- No paraprofessionals are observed in the classroom.

Interpretation

- The arrangement of the classroom is conducive for discussion. Students are able to see their classmates' faces when they are speaking.

- The teacher has established standards of conduct and the students understand her expectations for their behavior. When the teacher responds to misbehavior, the students comply with her request.

- It appears the students have previously brainstormed ideas for what to do when they are feeling frustrated. These strategies are posted on the wall.

- The students respond to the strategies the teacher uses for classroom management.

- For the most part, students are quiet and respectful when the teacher or another student is speaking during the first part of the video.

- Students' wiggling, fiddling in desk, turning around, etc. don't disrupt the environment as a whole. It appears these students are no longer fully engaged in the discussion activity.

Record of Evidence

Cluster 4: Student Intellectual Engagement
Guiding Questions
- *To what extent are students intellectually engaged in a classroom of high intellectual energy?*
- *What is the nature of what students are doing?*
- *Are they being challenged to think and make connections through both the instructional activities and the questions explored?*
- *Do the teacher's explanations of content correctly model academic language and invite intellectual work by students?*
- *Are students asked to explain their thinking, to construct logical arguments citing evidence, and to question the thinking of others?*
- *Are the instructional strategies used by the teacher suitable to the discipline, and to what extent do they promote student agency in the learning of challenging content?*

Evidence
- Students are on the fourth day of a story by Langston Hughes. The focus question is "Why does Mrs. Jones give Roger money for the blue suede shoes?" This is the first day the students have been asked to respond to this question.
- The teacher tells students at the beginning of the lesson that they are to directly respond to one another's ideas. Seldom does any student make reference to another student's comment. Most student comments are directed toward the teacher, not to other students.
- The teacher asks students to explain their reasoning and cite specific evidence, but only some students cite specific text evidence.
- Some students do not turn to the text when a student states the page number. Most do so when the teacher directs them to turn to a certain page number.
- The teacher attempts to scaffold the lesson with supporting questions, but few of the questions appear to help the students voice the motives behind the story's characters. Many student comments do not match the question asked.
- The teacher is inconsistent with asking probing questions of all students. There are times when students have difficulty answering the teacher's questions and she calls on another student without prodding to extend the learning of the student.
  - (1:20-2:00) S: She was teaching him a lesson before taking him outside to get his blue suede shoes. T: That's full of a lot of information. A lesson, first of all, what was the lesson and what makes you think she was trying to teach him a lesson? The student does not answer. T (without prodding the student): Does anyone agree with his answer? The teacher calls on another student.
  - The teacher rephrases her question at other times to prompt student learning. (19:50-22:39) A student reads a text, and after she begins sharing her understanding, pauses for a while. T (after a few moments): Are you rethinking your opinion? Okay, what has changed? S: Huh? T: "What has changed in your

Record of Evidence

Cluster 4: Student Intellectual Engagement

Evidence (cont'd.)

opinion since you reread that? The student is able to successfully answer after the teacher's prodding.
- The teacher anticipates in the lesson plan that it will take about 30 minutes to do the shared discussion activity. The shared discussion activity lasts about 46 minutes (1:10–47:00). Students appear to grow restless as the lesson progresses, yawning, stretching, and not turning to the page of the text being shared.
- Sometimes the teacher asks another question in a louder voice. This seems to increase the pressure to find the right evidence. It doesn't always lead to better results. Students are to share their logic as well as facts. The frustration in the classroom seems to build as the students have been searching for answers for quite a while at this point. Some students begin to talk over one another. The teacher turns her attention to the comments of interrupters, not to ask them to listen to their peers, but to listen to them.
- All activities are teacher-led. The discussion activity doesn't evolve into a discussion between students.

Record of Evidence

Cluster 4: Student Intellectual Engagement

Interpretation

- The teacher does not consistently require the students to respond directly to each other as outlined in the Five Guidelines for Shared Inquiry.

- Most students appear to be aware they are supposed to be citing evidence, but they have trouble both finding the evidence and linking their response to the question.

- The teacher does not consistently ask probing questions of all students to extend their learning when they answer incorrectly or do not answer at all.

- Not all students appear to be intellectually engaged throughout the lesson. Some students share their ideas freely during the class discussion. Others do not.

- The pacing structure of the lesson tends to drag during the discussion and be rushed during the two assessment activities, Building Your Answer journal page and Collaborative Assessment survey.

- Students participation is uneven. Some students participate more often than others.

- Near the end of the discussion, the teacher seems to abandon the guidelines she set at the beginning of the lesson.

Record of Evidence

Cluster 5: Successful Learning by All Students

Guiding Questions

- *To what extent does the teacher ensure learning by all students?*
- *Does the teacher monitor student understanding through specifically designed questions or instructional techniques?*
- *To what extent do students monitor their own learning and provide respectful feedback to classmates?*
- *Does the teacher make modifications in presentations or learning activities where necessary, taking into account the degree of student learning?*
- *Has the teacher sought out other resources (including parents) to support students' learning?*
- *In reflection, is the teacher aware of the success of the lesson in reaching students?*

Evidence

- Students are provided a focus question at the beginning of the class. The material has been read twice during the past two days. The focus question requires using reasoning in addition to textual evidence.
- Formative assessments include having the students write an opinion response to the Focus question before the discussion begins, and changing or standing by their opinion (in writing) near the end of the lesson. They are also to write a goal for their next discussion during the lesson closure. The teacher reads questions orally, but students must do their own writing. The teacher is circulating and monitoring students' progress during the time they are completing their assessment. She assists some students with the comments they are writing.
- The students will complete a summative assessment on the next day using a graphic organizer to record the evidence they found.
- The teacher monitors student learning by repeatedly asking the Focus question, "Why does Mrs. Jones give Roger money for the blue suede shoes?" She asks cluster questions she has listed in the lesson plan to extend students' learning during discussion and/or as follow-up questions. The teacher's use of the cluster questions is not successful in extending the learning of all students.
- The teacher is inconsistent when asking questions to extend students' learning. Some students who have difficulty answering the Focus question or Cluster Questions receive less prompting by the teacher than other students.
- The teacher writes notes on the seating chart during the lesson.
- Every student is invited to participate in a discussion to answer the focus question. Those that don't participate are given direct invitations using their name toward

Record of Evidence

Cluster 5: Successful Learning by All Students

Evidence (cont'd.)

  the end of the lesson. (1:14) T: I haven't heard from Kevin, would you like to join us? Arielle, join us?
- (39:00-40:03) T: We will go around and get a couple who have not spoken yet. We will start with you, Josia, since you said "me."
- (15:00) T: Any other answers to the focus question besides what I have heard so far?
- This lesson follows the protocol of the Great Books program. Students are to direct their comments to other students and cite evidence. Students are to give one another feedback during their discussion, but they rarely do so. A few students provide feedback to another student in the form of agreement or disagreement, and support their feedback by reading from the text. Students direct most of their comments to the teacher. When sharing about the Five Guidelines for Shared Inquiry discussion, the teacher says she is not to be answering questions, only posing them.
- (47:00-50:00) After the shared discussion activity, the teacher directs students to amend, change, or retain their original answer to the Focus question on their Building Your Answer journal page. The teacher monitors by walking around to examine students' work and providing feedback to some students. Students have three minutes to complete the Building Answer Form. All students do not finish in this time period.
- Of the five Building Your Answer student samples provided as artifacts, two students retain their original answer and three students change/amend their answer. Four of the students support their answer by quoting text. One student supports the initial answer by quoting text.
- (50:00) One student is asked to share her work on Building Your Answer. T: I notice that some of you have changed your response. Is there anyone here that would like to read your changed response and tell me why you changed your answer? She calls on Shania.
- S: I added on. I missed out on some details. In my new response I think Mrs. Jones gave Roger the money because after Mrs. Jones told Roger about her job and him seeing on the far side, I think she may have given Roger the money because she thought he had learned his lessons to not steal and to ask instead of take and to never do that again.
- Some students are unable to complete the Building Your Answer journal sheet during the three-minute period. Some students are still writing during the dialogue between the teacher and student.
- (56:00-57:34) The teacher tells the students to write down what they think their goal should be for the next time. She tells them she wants to know what they think about each of these areas and where there may be some improvement. One student's goal written on the Our Collaboration student sample states: "We sould [sic] keep up the place [sic] and make it more clearer like show it in a different

Record of Evidence

Cluster 5:   Successful Learning by All Students

Evidence (cont'd.)

way." This is taken directly as written on the survey. The word "place" is circled and "PACE" is written above it.
- The lesson plan and interview do not provide any information on communication with parents.
- The teacher interview does not contain a reflection on student learning that took place or how to adapt it to further promote student learning in the future. Ms. Jackson did express noticing that certain students who are seated closer to her and each other seem to be more comfortable. Their level of participation increases since such partnering promotes discussion of the focus question with one another.
- The teacher keeps a brief record of which students participate in the discussion, and she takes care to make certain each student speaks at least once. There is no evidence available about the teacher maintaining a coherent record-keeping system.

Interpretation

- The following day's summative assessment activity shows connection to the lesson.

- The cluster questions don't seem to be any more effective in helping students achieve higher-order cognitive functioning than the original focus question.

- The teacher attempts to ensure all students are called on to participate in the discussion. She makes marks on a seating chart to track students' participation.

- Most students do not give feedback directly to other students.

- The fact that only one student shares her answer from the Building Your Answer journal page may be due to lack of time for others to share.

- Some students are unable to complete the Building Your Answer journal sheet during the three-minute period. The last two assessment activities, Building Your Answer Journal Page and Our Collaboration Survey appear to be rushed.

- One student's thoughts about what the class goal should be for the next time appear to be credible for improvement of student collaboration.

- It is unclear if the teacher commentary took place before or after the lesson observation.

Record of Evidence

Cluster 6: Professionalism
Guiding Questions

- *To what extent does the teacher engage with the professional community (within the school and beyond) and demonstrate a commitment to ongoing professional learning?*

- *Does the teacher collaborate productively with colleagues and contribute to the life of the school?*

- *Does the teacher engage in professional learning and take a leadership role in the school to promote the welfare of students?*

Evidence

No evidence of Cluster 6 is present in this Instructional Set.

Looking at Teaching Through the Lens of the FFT Clusters

A Study Guide for Teacher Learning Communities

Teacher: Pierce
Subject: ELA
Grade: K
Topic: Taking Notes

Welcome to the Study Guide for the Pierce ELA Instructional Set, a collection of artifacts and videos for an instructional lesson. This Study Guide provides information and instructions on how to examine teaching and learning through the lens of the Framework for Teaching (FFT) Clusters. In order to complete the steps in this Guide, you will need access to the teacher's planning documents, the lesson video, and the teacher commentary video (http://www.danielsongroup.org/study-guides/). Steps 1–5 of this Study Guide focus on examining the Instructional Set and can be done by an individual. Step 6 is a group activity and focuses on sharing results of the analysis and applications of learning.

Step 1 - Lesson Overview

Read the background information of the lesson provided below.

This English Language Arts lesson is a research/informative writing lesson. Students have been reading to learn about communities and about jobs in the community in both Reading and Social Studies classes. Each student is now researching and writing about a job that he or she would like to know more about. These job choices were selected in a prior lesson. Students use multiple nonfiction books about nurses, doctors, police officers, firefighters, dentists, veterinarians, and pharmacists. The Pebble-go database is an additional resource students use to gain information about their chosen job.

Today's lesson includes reviews of how to work together in pairs or small groups, how to use resources to find information, and how to record the new information using pictures or labels. Students are using these previously-learned skills to gather new information from nonfiction texts: "Find the tools a specific community helper uses in his/her profession" and "What tools do they use? How do they use these tools?"

Students will write a draft of their information, working together in their group. Students use a Reading and Analyzing Nonfiction (RAN) chart to organize, gather, and sort information. They will write down new information found about their chosen job. Ms. Pierce mentions that students may add other information found along the way as they conduct research during today's lesson.

Students, grouped according to their job choices, are looking for new information about the tools he or she would use when performing his or her job, answering the question, "What tools does a _____ use to do his/her job?"

The teacher uses a nonfiction source about a teacher to review how to record a fact. She sketches a picture to collect information, including labels when applicable.

Group and individual RAN charts are completed as a whole-group activity. Sticky notes are placed within one of three sections to organize information learned about a particular job. The information is then personalized for the chosen jobs within small groups of two to three.

This lesson is aligned with two Common Core standards, with a focus on writing and participation:

- CCSS.ELA-Literacy.W.K.2 Use a combination of drawing, dictating, and writing to compose informative/explanatory texts in which they name what they are writing about and supply some information about the topic.

- CCSS.ELA-Literacy.W.K.7 Participate in shared research and writing projects.

Many other standards will be addressed in this lesson:

- CCSS.ELA-Literacy.RI.K.7 With prompting and support, describe the relationship between illustrations and the text in which they appear (e.g., what person, place, thing, or idea in the text an illustration depicts).

- CCSS.ELA-Literacy.RF.K.3 Know and apply grade-level phonics and word analysis skills in decoding words.

- CCSS.ELA-Literacy.RF.K.1 Demonstrate understanding of the organization and basic features of print.

- CCSS.ELA-Literacy.L.K.1a Print many upper- and lower-case letters.

- CCSS.ELA-Literacy.L.K.2c Write a letter or letters for most consonant and short-vowel sounds (phonemes).

- CCSS.ELA-Literacy.L.K.2d Spell simple words phonetically, drawing on knowledge of sound-letter relationships.

Ms. Pierce sequences the lesson from whole-group examples of researching tools to small-group examples. She has students draw the tools and place them within the tri-sectioned chart. The "Features of a Good Report" resource specifies facts and title, but also includes pictures. Pictures match the words and labels and guide group discussion.

In closing the lesson, students gather back on the carpet to share one piece of information that was discovered today.

Ms. Pierce reminds students that the information they gathered today will be published tomorrow for the final project. This process will continue until all research is completed.

Step 2 - Preparation and Questions

- *Read the teacher's lesson plan and jot down things you expect to see and what you want to look for in the video of the lesson.*

- *Write down any questions or comments you have about the lesson plan.*

Step 3 - Viewing the Classroom Video

- *View the complete video, noting those things you expected to see based on the lesson plan. Also note what was missing based on your expectations from the lesson plan. Jot down significant behaviors by the teacher and students pertinent to the FFT Clusters.*

Step 4 - Selected Highlights of the Lesson Video

Read the highlights of the lesson provided below. Note those matching your highlights of the lesson. For each set of statements, determine the FFT Cluster that is best related to the behaviors presented.

A. Students look for new information about the tools he or she would use when performing his or her job. "What tools does a _____ use to do his/her job?" The teacher reviews how to record a fact by using a nonfiction source about a teacher and by sketching a picture to collect information, and/or including labels when developmentally appropriate. (Cluster ____)

B. The teacher reviews the types of nonfiction sources available and demonstrates how to use each source to gather information. The teacher also reviews how to work together to gather information. (Cluster ____)

C. Ms. Pierce presents content and procedures to her "friends," explaining, defining, and reminding the class of terminology. She draws similarities between the new task and the teacher sample completed by the class previously. She demonstrates a new job (meteorologist) that Ms. Pierce wants to learn more about, while eliciting student assistance in discovering what is already known and what is yet to be learned about the profession. Example: Groundhog Day is a superstition that meteorologists might use as one of their tools. (Cluster ____)

D. Although today's focus is in on tools, students may add to other sections of their research if they find additional information along the way. Students are asked to share the names of tools as well as their use. (Cluster ____)

E. The teacher's explanation of content modeled academic language and invited intellectual work by students. Ms. Pierce encourages higher-level thinking skills and language (i.e., visual literacy, schema, nonfiction books). Language is appropriate for kindergarten levels of development; the atmosphere is business-like, with expectations for learning provided throughout. The teacher listens to students and builds on/uses their responses as she gives directions. (Cluster ____)

F. The content is scaffolded (e.g., review of what they have been doing, what they are doing today, and what they will do in the future), resulting in a clear pathway to completion. Teacher: "So what are you doing today? What book are you using? Where are you going to start? What are you looking for today?" (Cluster ____)

G. The teacher invites students to respond directly to one another's ideas, but few do so. Teacher: "Remember, you are to share in your group. You have to be close to each other to do that. You are to share the book." Teacher has them demonstrate how to sit close. (Cluster ____)

H. The physical environment is literacy-rich (e.g., pocket charts with vocabulary, books and computers on shelves, laminated KWL charts on students' desks). Routines and procedures are clear and carried out by both teacher and students with little loss of instructional time. Students move quickly and quietly from small-group interactions to whole-class discussion. (Cluster ____)

I. Students work together to research and draft the "tools" section of their project. Students are paired with another student to complete the research on one of the selected professions and share their findings with others. During this research project, the students use nonfiction text and computer resources which include facts, title, pictures, and matching words and labels. Many students share such information with others in their class, in small groups and with the teacher. (Cluster ____)

J. Ms. Pierce moves from table to table, talking with students as they work on their project, asking what they are doing, if they are following directions etc. She then moves on to the next table group. The teacher spends some time with one particular student who appears to have difficulty. Ms. Pierce practices phonetically with him to help him find the tools for his project. (Cluster ____)

> K. In closing the lesson, students gather back on the carpet to share one piece of information that was discovered today. Teacher reminds students that tomorrow, the information gathered today about "tools" will be published for the final project. (Cluster ____)

Step 5 – Viewing the Teacher Commentary

Watch the video of the teacher's commentary about the lesson and jot down any questions or comments you have about the commentary. Read the highlights below and identify the related FFT Cluster.

Ms. Pierce shares that students researched different jobs to discover facts about those jobs. Prior to today's lesson, they did a class research project on the job of a teacher. Today, students gathered around the tools of a variety of trades (i.e., stethoscope, ladder, radar gun, dog, and pencil & paper). Ms. Pierce selected texts that were rich in visual literacy so the students could pull the needed information. None of the books were from a series.

> A. Ms. Pierce shared two specific common core standards being emphasized within the lesson (research participation; and drawing, dictating, and writing). Many other standards were involved i.e., sounding out letters, and writing the letter either in lower or upper case.
> - CCSS.ELA-Literacy.W.K.2 Use a combination of drawing, dictating, and writing to compose informative/explanatory texts in which they name what they are writing about and supply some information about the topic.

- CCSS.ELA-Literacy.W.K.7 Participate in shared research and writing projects. (Cluster ___)

B. Most children in kindergarten cannot read, so Ms. Pierce selects books that are picture-rich so student who cannot read can see the pictures ("visual literacy piece"). (Cluster _)

C. Ms. Pierce notes that nonfiction text is appropriate for children in Kindergarten below or above grade level. Students above grade level are able to interact with both text and illustrations like we do as adults. Students at or above grade level can gather from the text or from the visuals. Paired students can gather and confirm the same information. (Cluster ___)

D. Ms. Pierce is encouraging the growth of understanding about a particular profession (i.e., the firefighter's use of ladders to help people). She is also challenging her students to reach for deeper understanding as she moves her students from merely receiving facts from the teacher toward implementing research skills to independently discover information using nonfiction texts. (Cluster ___)

Step 6 – Questions, Applications, and Discussion

The purpose of this step is to prompt your analysis and reflection of the Instructional Set and to have you think about applications to your own practice.

1. **Teaching and Learning Related to the FFT Clusters**

The purpose of the activity is to increase your understanding of the relationship between the highlights of the Instructional Set and the FFT Clusters. Your identification of an FFT Cluster for each of the highlights is compared to the Cluster identified by the master coders. The Answer Key is located at the end of the activities. You have options on how to complete the comparison.

Determine what might work best for your group's learning. Options include, but are not limited to the following.

- Look at the first set of highlights. Take a poll of what each group member identified as the related FFT Cluster. If all members said the same FFT Cluster, have one or two members say why. Compare the group's response to the answer sheet. Repeat for the remainder of the highlights.

OR

- Have each member take one or two highlights. State the correct answer for each one, and a reason why the highlight demonstrates that FFT Cluster. The member will facilitate a discussion if others had different responses, with the goal of having all understand the justification of the correct answer.

OR

- Have members check their own responses to all the highlights. If there are any incorrect answers, then the member selects one highlight and leads a discussion with the group to learn why others think the highlight matches the correct FFT Cluster.

OR

- Determine your own process to check and discuss the match between highlights and the FFT Clusters.

2. **Analysis and Reflection of the Instructional Set**

The purpose of this activity is for you to analyze and reflect on what you saw and heard in the artifacts and videos, to share your analysis with your peers, and to discuss some of the questions or comments you noted. Review the notes, comments, and questions you recorded when you examined the Instructional Set.

- Identify a key teaching and learning attribute demonstrated in the Instructional Set that was effective and state why you think it worked well.

- Identify a different attribute and provide ideas about how it could be enhanced or improved.

- Share your statements with your group and have your peers react to and build upon your analysis and ideas.

Sample statements:

I noticed that most of the students participated in the lesson today. One male student (investigating farmers) appeared not to have a partner, so couldn't participate in the collaborative part of the lesson. Additionally, I observed you assisting/working with him for part of the group time. I would want to know how you felt this student did today. I suggest you might want to adjust or modify your grouping of students to include him in a small group as it might benefit him in monitoring his behavior and in completing the assignment.

Additional ideas for statements:

- Degree that the instructional strategies, scaffolding, and materials and resources align with the goals and are appropriate for these students

- Extent to which the learning environment is safe for risk taking, and how that environment is established and maintained

- Extent to which students demonstrate a commitment to mastering challenging content. You know your students. Which students did you see persevere well in their research? Which students do you believe could have demonstrated a little more persistence? Can you think of a strategy you might try in the future to encourage their persistence when you observe some students quitting or giving up when met with challenges?

- Extent that teacher monitored student understanding and methods used

3. **Notice, Learn, and Apply**

The purpose of this activity is for you to reflect on what you learned from your analysis of the Instructional Set and to determine how you will apply it to your teaching.

- Complete the statements:
  "I noticed _____."
  (Insert one thing you noticed about the teacher or students.)

  "And I learned _____."
  (State what you learned related to what you noticed.)

  "I will apply what I learned by _____."
  (Provide example of how you will use what you learned in your own context.)

- Share your statements with your group. Have others react and add how they might apply what you noticed to their own teaching context.

Sample statement:

- I noticed a few students responding to one another's ideas.
- I learned that students need prompts to begin the conversation, to challenge their thinking, and to make connections.
- I will apply what I learned during this literacy lesson when challenging students' thinking and making connections to previous readings and discussions across various content areas.

Study Guide for Teachers Answer Key

Highlights from the Lesson Video (Step 4)

A. Students look for new information about the tools he or she would use when performing his or her job. "What tools does a _____ use to do his/her job?" The teacher reviews how to record a fact by using a nonfiction source about a teacher and by sketching a picture to collect information, and/or including labels when developmentally appropriate. (Cluster 4 Student Intellectual Engagement)

B. The teacher reviews the types of nonfiction sources available and demonstrates how to use each source to gather information. The teacher also reviews how to work together to gather information. (Cluster 1 Clarity of Instructional Purpose and Accuracy of Content)

C. Ms. Pierce presents content and procedures to her "friends," explaining, defining, and reminding the class of terminology. She draws similarities between the new task and the teacher sample completed by the class previously. She demonstrates a new job (meteorologist) that Ms. Pierce wants to learn more about, while eliciting student assistance in discovering what is already known and what is yet to be learned about the profession. Example: Groundhog Day is a superstition that meteorologists might use as one of their tools. (Cluster 1 Clarity of Instructional Purpose and Accuracy of Content)

D. Although today's focus is in on tools, students may add to other sections of their research if they find additional information along the way. Students are asked to share the names of tools as well as their use. (Cluster 4 Student Intellectual Engagement)

E. The teacher's explanation of content modeled academic language and invited intellectual work by students. Ms. Pierce encourages higher-level thinking skills and language (i.e., visual literacy, schema, nonfiction books). Language is appropriate for kindergarten levels of development; the atmosphere is business-like, with expectations for learning provided throughout. The teacher listens to students and builds on/uses their responses as she gives directions. (Cluster 2 Safe, Respectful, Supportive, and Challenging Learning Environment)

F. The content is scaffolded (e.g., review of what they have been doing, what they are doing today, and what they will do in the future), resulting in a clear pathway to completion. Teacher: "So what are you doing today? What book are you using? Where are you going to start? What are you looking for today?" (Cluster 4)

G. The teacher invites students to respond directly to one another's ideas, but few do so. Teacher: "Remember, you are to share in your group. You have to be close to each other to do that. You are to share the book." Teacher has them demonstrate how to sit close. (Cluster 4 Student Intellectual Engagement)

Study Guide for Teachers Answer Key

Highlights from the Lesson Video (Step 4—cont'd.)

H. The physical environment is literacy-rich (e.g., pocket charts with vocabulary, books and computers on shelves, laminated KWL charts on students' desks). Routines and procedures are clear and carried out by both teacher and students with little loss of instructional time. Students move quickly and quietly from small-group interactions to whole-class discussion. (Cluster 3 Classroom Management)

I. Students work together to research and draft the "tools" section of their project. Students are paired with another student to complete the research on one of the selected professions and share their findings with others. During this research project, the students use nonfiction text and computer resources which include facts, title, pictures, and matching words and labels. Many students share such information with others in their class, in small groups and with the teacher. (Cluster 4 Student Intellectual Engagement)

J. Ms. Pierce moves from table to table, talking with students as they work on their project, asking what they are doing, if they are following directions etc. She then moves on to the next table group. The teacher spends some time with one particular student who appears to have difficulty. Ms. Pierce practices phonetically with him to help him find the tools for his project. (Cluster 5 Successful Learning by All Students)

K. In closing the lesson, students gather back on the carpet to share one piece of information that was discovered today. Teacher reminds students that tomorrow, the information gathered today about "tools" will be published for the final project. (Cluster 4 Student Intellectual Engagement)

Study Guide for Teachers Answer Key

Highlights from the Teacher Commentary (Step 5)

A. Ms. Pierce shared two specific common core standards being emphasized within the lesson (research participation; and drawing, dictating, and writing). Many other standards were involved i.e., sounding out letters, and writing the letter either in lower or upper case.

- CCSS.ELA-Literacy.W.K.2 Use a combination of drawing, dictating, and writing to compose informative/explanatory texts in which they name what they are writing about and supply some information about the topic.
- CCSS.ELA-Literacy.W.K.7 Participate in shared research and writing projects. (Cluster 1 Clarity of Instructional Purpose and Accuracy of Content)

B. Most children in kindergarten cannot read, so Ms. Pierce selects books that are picture-rich so student who cannot read can see the pictures ("visual literacy piece"). (Cluster 1 Clarity of Instructional Purpose and Accuracy of Content)

C. Ms. Pierce notes that nonfiction text is appropriate for children in Kindergarten below or above grade level. Students above grade level are able to interact with both text and illustrations like we do as adults. Students at or above grade level can gather from the text or from the visuals. Paired students can gather and confirm the same information. (Cluster 1 Clarity of Instructional Purpose and Accuracy of Content)

D. Ms. Pierce is encouraging the growth of understanding about a particular profession (i.e., the firefighter's use of ladders to help people). She is also challenging her students to reach for deeper understanding as she moves her students from merely receiving facts from the teacher toward implementing research skills to independently discover information using nonfiction texts. (Cluster 4 Student Intellectual Engagement)

**Looking at Teaching Through
the Lens of the FFT Clusters**

A Study Guide for
Instructional Coach
Learning Communities

Teacher: Pierce
Subject: ELA
Grade: K
Topic: Taking Notes

Welcome to the Study Guide for the Pierce ELA Instructional Set, a collection of artifacts and videos for an instructional lesson. This Study Guide provides information and instructions on how to examine teaching and learning through the lens of the Framework for Teaching (FFT) Clusters. In order to complete the steps in this Guide, you will need access to the teacher's planning documents, the lesson video, and the teacher commentary video (http://www.danielsongroup.org/study-guides/). Steps 1–5 of this Study Guide focus on examining the Instructional Set and can be done by an individual. Step 6 is a group activity and focuses on sharing results of the analysis and applications of learning.

Step 1 - Lesson Overview

Read the background information of the lesson provided below.

This English Language Arts lesson is a research/informative writing lesson. Students have been reading to learn about communities and about jobs in the community in both Reading and Social Studies classes. Each student is now researching and writing about a job that he or she would like to know more about. These job choices were selected in a prior lesson. Students use multiple nonfiction books about nurses, doctors, police officers, firefighters, dentists, veterinarians, and pharmacists. The Pebble-go database is an additional resource students use to gain information about their chosen job.

Today's lesson includes reviews of how to work together in pairs or small groups, how to use resources to find information, and how to record the new information using pictures or labels. Students are using these previously-learned skills to gather new information from nonfiction texts: "Find the tools a specific community helper uses in his/her profession" and "What tools do they use? How do they use these tools?"

Students will write a draft of their information, working together in their group. Students use a Reading and Analyzing Nonfiction (RAN) chart to organize, gather, and sort information. They will write down new information found about their chosen job. Ms. Pierce mentions that students may add other information found along the way as they conduct research during today's lesson.

Students, grouped according to their job choices, are looking for new information about the tools he or she would use when performing his or her job, answering the question, "What tools does a _____ use to do his/her job?"

The teacher uses a nonfiction source about a teacher to review how to record a fact. She sketches a picture to collect information, including labels when applicable.

Group and individual RAN charts are completed as a whole-group activity. Sticky notes are placed within one of three sections to organize information learned about a particular job. The information is then personalized for the chosen jobs within small groups of two to three.

This lesson is aligned with two Common Core standards, with a focus on writing and participation:

- CCSS.ELA-Literacy.W.K.2 Use a combination of drawing, dictating, and writing to compose informative/explanatory texts in which they name what they are writing about and supply some information about the topic.

- CCSS.ELA-Literacy.W.K.7 Participate in shared research and writing projects.

Many other standards will be addressed in this lesson:

- CCSS.ELA-Literacy.RI.K.7 With prompting and support, describe the relationship between illustrations and the text in which they appear (e.g., what person, place, thing, or idea in the text an illustration depicts).

- CCSS.ELA-Literacy.RF.K.3 Know and apply grade-level phonics and word analysis skills in decoding words.

- CCSS.ELA-Literacy.RF.K.1 Demonstrate understanding of the organization and basic features of print.

- CCSS.ELA-Literacy.L.K.1a Print many upper- and lower-case letters.

- CCSS.ELA-Literacy.L.K.2c Write a letter or letters for most consonant and short-vowel sounds (phonemes).

- CCSS.ELA-Literacy.L.K.2d Spell simple words phonetically, drawing on knowledge of sound-letter relationships.

Ms. Pierce sequences the lesson from whole-group examples of researching tools to small-group examples. She has students draw the tools and place them within the tri-sectioned chart. The "Features of a Good Report" resource specifies facts and title, but also includes pictures. Pictures match the words and labels and guide group discussion.

In closing the lesson, students gather back on the carpet to share one piece of information that was discovered today.

Ms. Pierce reminds students that the information they gathered today will be published tomorrow for the final project. This process will continue until all research is completed.

Step 2 - Preparation and Questions

- Read the teacher's lesson plan and jot down things you expect to see and what you want to look for in the video of the lesson.

- Write down any questions or comments you have about the lesson plan.

Step 3 – Viewing the Classroom Video

- View the complete video, noting those things you expected to see based on the lesson plan. Also note what was missing based on your expectations from the lesson plan. Jot down significant behaviors by the teacher and students pertinent to the FFT Clusters.

Step 4 – Selected Highlights of the Lesson Video

Read the highlights of the lesson provided below. Note those matching your highlights of the lesson. For each set of statements, determine the FFT Cluster that is best related to the behaviors presented.

A. Students look for new information about the tools he or she would use when performing his or her job. "What tools does a _____ use to do his/her job?" The teacher reviews how to record a fact by using a nonfiction source about a teacher and by sketching a picture to collect information, and/or including labels when developmentally appropriate. (Cluster ____)

B. The teacher reviews the types of nonfiction sources available and demonstrates how to use each source to gather information. The teacher also reviews how to work together to gather information. (Cluster ____)

C. Ms. Pierce presents content and procedures to her "friends," explaining, defining, and reminding the class of terminology. She draws similarities between the new task and the teacher sample completed by the class previously. She demonstrates a new job (meteorologist) that Ms. Pierce wants to learn more about, while eliciting student assistance in discovering what is already known and what is yet to be learned about the profession. Example: Groundhog Day is a superstition that meteorologists might use as one of their tools. (Cluster ____)

D. Although today's focus is in on tools, students may add to other sections of their research if they find additional information along the way. Students are asked to share the names of tools as well as their use. (Cluster ____)

E. The teacher's explanation of content modeled academic language and invited intellectual work by students. Ms. Pierce encourages higher-level thinking skills and language (i.e., visual literacy, schema, nonfiction books). Language is appropriate for kindergarten levels of development; the atmosphere is business-like, with expectations for learning provided throughout. The teacher listens to students and builds on/uses their responses as she gives directions. (Cluster ____)

F. The content is scaffolded (e.g., review of what they have been doing, what they are doing today, and what they will do in the future), resulting in a clear pathway to completion. Teacher: "So what are you doing today? What book are you using? Where are you going to start? What are you looking for today?" (Cluster ____)

G. The teacher invites students to respond directly to one another's ideas, but few do so. Teacher: "Remember, you are to share in your group. You have to be close to each other to do that. You are to share the book." Teacher has them demonstrate how to sit close. (Cluster ____)

H. The physical environment is literacy-rich (e.g., pocket charts with vocabulary, books and computers on shelves, laminated KWL charts on students' desks). Routines and procedures are clear and carried out by both teacher and students with little loss of instructional time. Students move quickly and quietly from small-group interactions to whole-class discussion. (Cluster ____)

I. Students work together to research and draft the "tools" section of their project. Students are paired with another student to complete the research on one of the selected professions and share their findings with others. During this research project, the students use nonfiction text and computer resources which include facts, title, pictures, and matching words and labels. Many students share such information with others in their class, in small groups and with the teacher. (Cluster ____)

J. Ms. Pierce moves from table to table, talking with students as they work on their project, asking what they are doing, if they are following directions etc. She then moves on to the next table group. The teacher spends some time with one particular student who appears to have difficulty. Ms. Pierce practices phonetically with him to help him find the tools for his project. (Cluster ____)

K. In closing the lesson, students gather back on the carpet to share one piece of information that was discovered today. Teacher reminds students that tomorrow, the information gathered today about "tools" will be published for the final project. (Cluster ____)

Step 5 – Viewing the Teacher Commentary

Watch the video of the teacher's commentary about the lesson and jot down any questions or comments you have about the commentary. Read the highlights below and identify the related FFT Cluster.

Ms. Pierce shares that students researched different jobs to discover facts about those jobs. Prior to today's lesson, they did a class research project on the job of a teacher. Today, students gathered around the tools of a variety of trades (i.e., stethoscope, ladder, radar gun, dog, and pencil & paper). Ms. Pierce selected texts that were rich in visual literacy so the students could pull the needed information. None of the books were from a series.

A. Ms. Pierce shared two specific common core standards being emphasized within the lesson (research participation; and drawing, dictating, and writing). Many other standards were involved i.e., sounding out letters, and writing the letter either in lower or upper case.
   - CCSS.ELA-Literacy.W.K.2 Use a combination of drawing, dictating, and writing to compose informative/explanatory texts in which they name what they are writing about and supply some information about the topic.

> - CCSS.ELA-Literacy.W.K.7 Participate in shared research and writing projects. (Cluster ___)
>
> B. Most children in kindergarten cannot read, so Ms. Pierce selects books that are picture-rich so student who cannot read can see the pictures ("visual literacy piece"). (Cluster _)
>
> C. Ms. Pierce notes that nonfiction text is appropriate for children in Kindergarten below or above grade level. Students above grade level are able to interact with both text and illustrations like we do as adults. Students at or above grade level can gather from the text or from the visuals. Paired students can gather and confirm the same information. (Cluster ___)
>
> D. Ms. Pierce is encouraging the growth of understanding about a particular profession (i.e., the firefighter's use of ladders to help people). She is also challenging her students to reach for deeper understanding as she moves her students from merely receiving facts from the teacher toward implementing research skills to independently discover information using nonfiction texts. (Cluster ___)

Step 6 – Questions, Applications, and Discussion

The purpose of this step is to prompt your analysis and reflection of the Instructional Set and to have you think about applications to your own practice.

1. **Teaching and Learning Related to the FFT Clusters**

The purpose of the activity is to increase your understanding of the relationship between the highlights of the Instructional Set and the FFT Clusters. Your identification of an FFT Cluster for each of the highlights is compared to the Cluster identified by the master coders. The Answer Key is located at the end of the activities. You have options on how to complete the comparison. Determine what might work best for your group's learning. Options include, but are not limited to the following.

- Look at the first set of highlights. Take a poll of what each group member identified as the related FFT Cluster. If all members said the same FFT Cluster, then have one or two members say why. Compare the group's response to the answer sheet. Repeat for the remainder of the sets of highlights.

OR

- Have each member take one or two sets of highlights and be the discussant for them. The discussant will state the correct answer and state a reason why the statements in the set demonstrate the FFT Cluster. The discussant will facilitate a discussion if members had different responses with the goal of all understanding the justification of the correct answer.

OR

- Have members check their own responses to all the sets of highlights. If there are any incorrect answers, then the member selects one set and leads a discussion with the group to learn why others think the highlights match the correct FFT Cluster.

OR

- Determine your own process to check and discuss the match between highlights and the FFT Clusters.

2. **Analysis and Reflection of the Instructional Set**

The purpose of this activity is for you to analyze and reflect on what you saw and heard in the artifacts and videos and to discuss some of the questions or comments you noted. One element of a professional conversation is asking questions to ascertain more information about a teacher's thinking and the behaviors of both students and teacher. This activity allows you and your peers to practice preparing such questions. Your peers can comment on whether your questions are appropriate and will obtain useful information without making the featured teacher feel uneasy or criticized.

The second part of this activity focuses on helping teachers move their practice forward. Please note that having you prepare for and model an entire conversation about the lesson with the featured teacher is not the purpose of this activity as written. Your group can modify or replace the activity to meet your group's needs

- Review the notes, comments, and questions you recorded when you examined the Instructional Set. Pretend you have the opportunity to ask the teacher some questions to get additional information about the strategies used or decisions made for this Instructional Set.

- Share with your group just the questions you would use with the teacher to elicit additional information. Have your peers comment about your questions and add other questions they had about the same event.

- Share with others in your group what you would do to prompt the teacher's thinking and actions to enhance his/her practice. Take turns sharing and discussing the prompts.

Sample A, Part I:

You did a wonderful job of getting the students engaged in researching and writing about a job that he or she would like to know more about. Students were grouped according to their job choices. They were looking for new information about the tools someone would use when performing his or her job to answer the question "What tools does a _____ use to do his/her job?"

It is my perception that the students looked to you to orchestrate the interactions. How might you plan for the students to respond to each other? What criteria would you need to teach, so that students might be ready to ask questions of other students?

Sample A, Part II:

I know it is something of a challenge, but I think there were a few students in your class who, if given the prompt, would ask question of their peers. How might rotating the role of discussion facilitator help sustain the discussion by the students (with some teacher interjections at critical spots)? What knowledge or skill might students need for them to be able to facilitate the discussion? How might you go about teaching that knowledge or skill? What might you as a teacher use as criteria to determine when to interject?

Sample B, Part I:

You demonstrated the importance of participation in shared research and writing projects for this lesson. For example, you grouped students who gathered information about their "tools" either through the texts provided or visuals. I am wondering what procedures need to be taught prior to a lesson so most of the students could self-direct their learning, explain their reasoning, and cite specific text/visuals. What evidence might students be showing you that demonstrate they responded to one another's work?

Sample B, Part II:

As you return to the process of group participation and gathering information in tomorrow's lesson focused on "Tools of the Trade," what might you do to prompt and support student grouping, student thinking, and discussion? When do you think it might have been a good time to transition them into the deeper exploration? What do you pay attention to that signals when it is a good time to transition into deeper exploration? What criteria might be used to discern when transitioning would be appropriate? What are some strategies you might use to initiate that transition?

3. **Notice, Learn, and Apply**

The purpose of this activity is for you to reflect on what you learned from your analysis of the Instructional Set and to determine how you will apply it to your teaching.

- Complete the statements:
  "I noticed _____."
  (Insert one thing you noticed about the teacher or students.)

  "And I learned _____."
  (State what you learned related to what you noticed.)

  "I will apply what I learned by _____."
  (Provide example of how you will use what you learned in your own context.)

- Share your statements with your group. Have others react and add how they might apply what you noticed to their own coaching context.

Sample statements:

- I noticed this lesson was not self-directed, as only a few students responded to one another's ideas.

- I learned that teachers need to model those procedures so that students understand how they can self-direct their learning.

- I will apply what I learned during this literacy lesson when planning to support students to self-direct their learning in readings and discussions across various content areas. I will share this strategy with other teachers that I'm coaching. I think this strategy will also work for teachers of math and science where students also can direct their own learning.

Study Guide for Instructional Coaches Answer Key
Highlights from the Lesson Video (Step 4)

A. Students look for new information about the tools he or she would use when performing his or her job. "What tools does a _____ use to do his/her job?" The teacher reviews how to record a fact by using a nonfiction source about a teacher and by sketching a picture to collect information, and/or including labels when developmentally appropriate. (Cluster 4 Student Intellectual Engagement)

B. The teacher reviews the types of nonfiction sources available and demonstrates how to use each source to gather information. The teacher also reviews how to work together to gather information. (Cluster 1 Clarity of Instructional Purpose and Accuracy of Content)

C. Ms. Pierce presents content and procedures to her "friends," explaining, defining, and reminding the class of terminology. She draws similarities between the new task and the teacher sample completed by the class previously. She demonstrates a new job (meteorologist) that Ms. Pierce wants to learn more about, while eliciting student assistance in discovering what is already known and what is yet to be learned about the profession. Example: Groundhog Day is a superstition that meteorologists might use as one of their tools. (Cluster 1 Clarity of Instructional Purpose and Accuracy of Content)

D. Although today's focus is in on tools, students may add to other sections of their research if they find additional information along the way. Students are asked to share the names of tools as well as their use. (Cluster 4 Student Intellectual Engagement)

E. The teacher's explanation of content modeled academic language and invited intellectual work by students. Ms. Pierce encourages higher-level thinking skills and language (i.e., visual literacy, schema, nonfiction books). Language is appropriate for kindergarten levels of development; the atmosphere is business-like, with expectations for learning provided throughout. The teacher listens to students and builds on/uses their responses as she gives directions. (Cluster 2 Safe, Respectful, Supportive, and Challenging Learning Environment)

F. The content is scaffolded (e.g., review of what they have been doing, what they are doing today, and what they will do in the future), resulting in a clear pathway to completion. Teacher: "So what are you doing today? What book are you using? Where are you going to start? What are you looking for today?" (Cluster 4)

G. The teacher invites students to respond directly to one another's ideas, but few do so. Teacher: "Remember, you are to share in your group. You have to be close to each other to do that. You are to share the book." Teacher has them demonstrate how to sit close. (Cluster 4 Student Intellectual Engagement)

Study Guide for Instructional Coaches Answer Key
Highlights from the Lesson Video (Step 4—cont'd.)

H. The physical environment is literacy-rich (e.g., pocket charts with vocabulary, books and computers on shelves, laminated KWL charts on students' desks). Routines and procedures are clear and carried out by both teacher and students with little loss of instructional time. Students move quickly and quietly from small-group interactions to whole-class discussion. (Cluster 3 Classroom Management)

I. Students work together to research and draft the "tools" section of their project. Students are paired with another student to complete the research on one of the selected professions and share their findings with others. During this research project, the students use nonfiction text and computer resources which include facts, title, pictures, and matching words and labels. Many students share such information with others in their class, in small groups and with the teacher. (Cluster 4 Student Intellectual Engagement)

J. Ms. Pierce moves from table to table, talking with students as they work on their project, asking what they are doing, if they are following directions etc. She then moves on to the next table group. The teacher spends some time with one particular student who appears to have difficulty. Ms. Pierce practices phonetically with him to help him find the tools for his project. (Cluster 5 Successful Learning by All Students)

K. In closing the lesson, students gather back on the carpet to share one piece of information that was discovered today. Teacher reminds students that tomorrow, the information gathered today about "tools" will be published for the final project. (Cluster 4 Student Intellectual Engagement)

Study Guide for Instructional Coaches Answer Key

Highlights from the Teacher Commentary (Step 5)

A. Ms. Pierce shared two specific common core standards being emphasized within the lesson (research participation; and drawing, dictating, and writing). Many other standards were involved i.e., sounding out letters, and writing the letter either in lower or upper case.

- CCSS.ELA-Literacy.W.K.2 Use a combination of drawing, dictating, and writing to compose informative/explanatory texts in which they name what they are writing about and supply some information about the topic.
- CCSS.ELA-Literacy.W.K.7 Participate in shared research and writing projects. (Cluster 1 Clarity of Instructional Purpose and Accuracy of Content)

B. Most children in kindergarten cannot read, so Ms. Pierce selects books that are picture-rich so student who cannot read can see the pictures ("visual literacy piece"). (Cluster 1 Clarity of Instructional Purpose and Accuracy of Content)

C. Ms. Pierce notes that nonfiction text is appropriate for children in Kindergarten below or above grade level. Students above grade level are able to interact with both text and illustrations like we do as adults. Students at or above grade level can gather from the text or from the visuals. Paired students can gather and confirm the same information. (Cluster 1 Clarity of Instructional Purpose and Accuracy of Content)

D. Ms. Pierce is encouraging the growth of understanding about a particular profession (i.e., the firefighter's use of ladders to help people). She is also challenging her students to reach for deeper understanding as she moves her students from merely receiving facts from the teacher toward implementing research skills to independently discover information using nonfiction texts. (Cluster 4 Student Intellectual Engagement)

Record of Evidence

This Record of Evidence (ROE) contains key evidence aligned to the FFT Clusters. Interpretive statements about the evidence are also provided. The ROE was created by two master coders who recorded evidence and interpretation statements independently, reviewed each others' work, and arrived at a final composite version based on their professional conversations. This version was reviewed by a leader of the master coders. The ROE is included in this Study Guide so users can see what master coders identified as key evidence, and their interpretation of that evidence through the lens of the FFT Clusters. It is provided as an example of one type of analysis of an Instructional Set. The ROEs were created for professional development rather than evaluative purposes. Users are cautioned about using them for teacher evaluation.

Rubric:	Generic
Grade:	K
Subject:	ELA
Topic:	Taking Notes
Teacher description:	Teacher is white, female; paraprofessional is African American, female
Class description:	18 students, 11 female, 7 male; approx. 5 may be African American.
Artifacts:	• Student work sample • Lesson plan • Teacher commentary
Length of video:	40:04

Record of Evidence

Cluster 1: Clarity of Instructional Purpose and Accuracy of Content

Guiding Questions

- *To what extent does the teacher demonstrate depth of important content knowledge and conduct the class with a clear and ambitious purpose, reflective of the standards for the discipline and appropriate to the students' levels of knowledge and skill?*

- *To what degree are the elements of a lesson (the sequence of topics, instructional strategies, and materials and resources) well designed and executed, and aligned with the purpose of the lesson?*

- *To what extent are they designed to engage students in high-level learning in the discipline?*

Evidence

Instructional Plan
- Teacher describes lesson as research/informative writing lesson. Students have been reading about jobs in the community in Reading and Social Studies. Each student has chosen a job they are interested in.
- Texts used include multiple nonfiction books, Pebble-go database.
- Common Core standards addressed: 2 Literacy (specific) and 6 others (all literacy standards dealing with spelling, writing, researching, word analysis).
- Teacher uses narrative to describe the agenda for the lesson.
- Preparation before today's lesson included working with nonfiction text on topic for four weeks; doing a class project; using a RAN chart to organize, gather, and sort information; grouping students according to their job choices; and writing down what they knew about the job.
- Today's lesson is looking for new information about tools. It will include a review of how to record information, including labels; a review of sources of information; and how to work together.
- Students will write a draft of their information, working together in their group.
- Teacher mentions that students may add other information found along the way as they research. She plans to bring students back to whole group on the carpet to share one piece of information they found, and preview tomorrow's work to publish the information gathered today. A future lesson will continue the process until the research is completed.

Video
- Teacher begins lesson by telling students they will continue to work on their research project. Teacher says that today they will talk about features of a great report. She refers to a poster they made after talking about really good nonfiction writing.

Record of Evidence

Cluster 1: **Clarity of Instructional Purpose and Accuracy of Content**

Evidence (cont'd.)

- Teacher speaks slowly and deliberately.
- Teacher asks students to tell her what they are working on today (facts).
- Teacher reviews what they have done so far. T: Today, we are going to answer the question, "What tools does a _____ use?"
- Teacher tells students she expects them to share one thing they learned today about tools.

Teacher Commentary
- This is an extension of students' unit (integration). Prior to this lesson, there was a class project (the job of a teacher). Texts were not part of any other series.
- This lesson addresses two standards: one is for writing, and one is for participation. There are many other standards involved. Teacher describes all the standards that the lesson targeted.
- In the past, the teacher did the reading, but with the Common Core, the children are doing more of the work.
- The one student work sample provided shows a handwritten statement from a student about what nurses use, and a picture of several nurse's tools.

Interpretation

- Lesson plan does not indicate a method for assessing student work.
- Several standards are addressed in the lesson plan.
- Information about students in the class is provided, however, the information is generic in nature (e.g., no identification of the ELL students or the students on an IEP).

Record of Evidence

Cluster 2: Safe, Respectful, Supportive, and Challenging Learning Environment

Guiding Questions

- *To what extent do the interactions between teacher and students, and among students, demonstrate genuine caring and a safe, respectful, supportive, and also challenging learning environment?*
- *Do teachers convey high expectations for student learning and encourage hard work and perseverance? Is the environment safe for risk taking?*
- *Do students take pride in their work and demonstrate a commitment to mastering challenging content?*

Evidence

- Teacher reminds students about a nonfiction report they wrote about ___? Students respond: Teachers.
- Teacher asks them to compare their report to the features listed on the chart to see if they have a really good report.
- Teacher calls on students by name, and calls them "friends."
- T: Now we know that Ms. Pierce is a pretty good reader. We know that some of us are pretty good readers too, but if I can't read this, where can I get the information?
- T (after student can't respond): Do you want me to come back to you?
- T: Ms. Pierce is going to draw that circle because Josh said that groundhogs come out of the ground. So, I'm going to draw a circle, and then I'm going to draw… it's not going to look like a good groundhog, but I'm gonna draw like the shape of something…. (Students excitedly offer ideas, teacher makes goofy face). Remember when we are working with our partners today, we have to stay at that level one (in louder, excited voice), even if what we find is so exciting, we want to yell! (Teacher talks quietly) It still has to be that level one, OK?
- T: You are going to try to find information about the tools, but if you have extra information, you can write that down too.
- T: Remember we are trying to share with our group, right? To make sure. So make sure that ___ sees that too.
- Teacher takes a pencil to another table to give to female student.
- T: You don't have to wait for him. You can get started without him if you want to. I like the fact that you are waiting on him though.
- T: I know you are finding some really great facts. I can hear your conversations.
- Teacher tells students they have two more minutes to do their research.

Record of Evidence

Cluster 2: Safe, Respectful, Supportive, and Challenging Learning Environment

Evidence (cont'd.)

- Teacher compliments student on his picture and reads the sentence; then compliments another student on his picture.
- T: We're gonna stop in two minutes. I know you like to do this.

Interpretation

- Language is suited to kindergarten levels of development.
- The teacher is friendly, but not overly so. The atmosphere is business-like, with expectations for learning provided throughout.
- The teacher listens to students and builds on/uses their responses as she gives directions.
- No disrespect is noted.

Record of Evidence

Cluster 3: Classroom Management

Guiding Questions

- *Is the classroom well run and organized?*
- *Are classroom routines and procedures clear and carried out efficiently by both teacher and students with little loss of instructional time?*
- *To what extent do students themselves take an active role in their smooth operation?*
- *Are directions for activities clearly explained so that there is no confusion?*
- *Do students not only understand and comply with standards of conduct, but also play an active part in setting the tone for maintaining those standards?*
- *How does the physical environment support the learning activities?*

Evidence

- Classroom is a visually rich environment. There is a carpeted area on the side of the room. Books are visible on shelves. Tables in groups of six have room for movement between them. Pocket charts are near teacher's chair in the reading area. Laminated charts and colored sticky notes are available for students. Materials and computers are on shelves around the room. Book bags and coats are hung up. Alphabet chart is on the wall. Students are seated on the carpet and move to tables when directed. Another adult is working with students throughout the lesson.
- Students are seated close to each other on a carpeted area with teacher in a chair in front of them.
- Teacher thanks a student (Sebastian) for raising his hand.
- T: How many of you think that you can go back to your spot and work with your partners to gather information? (Several students raise hands) Many friends do. Can you tell me, how are you going to sit with your partners to gather information? Sebastian?
- T: Umm, should Layla sit way over there and Ms. Pierce sit way over here if we're partners? Students: No. T: How should we sit then? Kimberly, thank you for the quiet thumb.
- Teacher has student come forward to model how to sit in a small group.
- T: What level are you going to be using? Students raise hands.
- T: Javen, what level is that? S: One. T: A one. Who can remind us what does a one sound like? Students whisper and teacher nods her head.
- One female student remains on the carpet after most of the students have gone to their seats for small group work; paraprofessional goes to student and urges her to move to the table area.
- Teacher pats a student and has her sit down, then moves back to student and kneels beside him.
- Teacher calls each group by "job" to go to their desks.

Record of Evidence

Cluster 3: Classroom Management

Evidence (cont'd.)

- Students talk to each other at tables and pull out materials from the center of the table.
- Students speak in quiet voices throughout the segment.
- Student wiggles, and writes on his chair with the eraser end of his pencil, unnoticed by other students.
- Teacher uses countdown to get students' attention when needed, and reminds students they need to be at level one so that they can hear the computers.
- T: Jocavic just found something and I forgot to tell you that I did this. Remember yesterday, when everybody kept looking for new post-it notes? Ms. Pierce has post-it notes on your hand charts if you need it, so that you have post-it notes on the front, OK?
- Teacher gives directions for putting things away; when teacher starts to talk, a student says something, and teacher says, "Stop," then continues with directions about putting things away, and coming to the carpet.
- Teacher compliments students who follow directions (calling them by name and stating what they are doing). The rest of the students come to the carpet with no talking.

Interpretation

- No misbehavior is observed.
- Correct behavior is modeled
- Materials are available (texts, computers, charts at tables, sticky notes).

Record of Evidence

Cluster 4: Student Intellectual Engagement

Guiding Questions

- To what extent are students intellectually engaged in a classroom of high intellectual energy?
- What is the nature of what students are doing?
- Are they being challenged to think and make connections through both the instructional activities and the questions explored?
- Do the teacher's explanations of content correctly model academic language and invite intellectual work by students?
- Are students asked to explain their thinking, to construct logical arguments citing evidence, and to question the thinking of others?
- Are the instructional strategies used by the teacher suitable to the discipline, and to what extent do they promote student agency in the learning of challenging content?

Evidence

- Teacher asks students if they included facts in their research about teachers.
- T: And where did we get those facts? S: Our schema. Teacher puts up KWL chart.
- T: Where did we go to find out if what we thought, we knew? Our schema, right?
- Jason: Books. Teacher reminds students that they also used the computer and the SmartBoard to find information; teacher follows the same procedure for each item that describes the features of a great report.
- Teacher models, using her interest in meteorologists.
- Teacher asks students how to confirm her schema. S: Go to school.
- Thomas: Look at the pictures. T: Remember, that's called "visual literacy." We're gonna use our pictures to gather information. Teacher shows them a picture in her book and asks what it is.
- Teacher talks to students about a Table of Contents.
- S: There's an audience. T: Good word choice.
- Teacher reads from the book about superstitions. T: So, could that be a tool?
- Teacher writes down the word "because that's a new fact that they're telling me." Teacher writes the word and asks students to help her with the phonetic sounds. One student says, "it's 'ow' or 'ou.'" Teacher: Nice job, Layla.
- T: OK, that picture's gonna help me remember what I wrote, especially if I didn't sound it out all the way. So where does that go? Is that a "what do we think we know?" Students: No. T: No. Is it a "yes, we were right?" Students: No. T: Is that a "new fact?" Students: Yes. Teacher places sticky note on the chart in the last column.
- T: So on your chart, when you find new facts today, you're going to put your new facts in that last column where it says, "new facts." Now, I want to show you one more because I found something cool. Teacher turns pages in a book.

Record of Evidence

Cluster 4: Student Intellectual Engagement

Evidence (cont'd.)

- T: Remember you are to share in your group. You have to be close to each other to do that.
- When students are working with their group, teacher repeatedly asks questions such as "So what are you doing today? What book are you using? Where are you going to start? What are you looking for today?"
- T: Remember, we are to share with our group.
- T: What is that thing for? S: It's a measuring thing. T: Ooh, to measure how tall you are or short you are? S: Inaudible. T: What else does it measure besides that? It measures how much you.... (teacher puts hands to waist). S: Weigh. T: Right, how much you weigh. (Teacher points to picture) T: It's called a scale, that's what. So you can draw a picture or you can write the word. Is that a tool that doctors use? Student responds, and teacher nods her head. T: Right.
- T: OK? I'm bringing more of them (computers) around. Keep working.
- Teacher asks two girls what tools they have found. They tell her they haven't found any yet, and she reminds them to be sure they are looking for tools. She opens another computer and puts it on the table for the girls.
- Teacher talks about three professions using the same tool (stethoscope); nurses, doctors, veterinarians.

Interpretation

- Content is scaffolded. Teacher reviews what they have been doing, what they are doing today, and what they will do in the future.

- Activity is modeled.

- The teacher reminds students multiple times that they are to work together, and that they are to look for tools. The conversations with each group are about what students are doing, not necessarily about what they are learning.

- Students use challenging academic vocabulary, e.g., "schema," "audience."

Record of Evidence

Cluster 5:   Successful Learning by All Students
Guiding Questions

- *To what extent does the teacher ensure learning by all students?*
- *Does the teacher monitor student understanding through specifically designed questions or instructional techniques?*
- *To what extent do students monitor their own learning and provide respectful feedback to classmates?*
- *Does the teacher make modifications in presentations or learning activities where necessary, taking into account the degree of student learning?*
- *Has the teacher sought out other resources (including parents) to support students' learning?*
- *In reflection, is the teacher aware of the success of the lesson in reaching students?*

Evidence

Lesson plan
- Teacher lists 23 students, 3 with IEP, 9 ELL, 8 students low-income.
- No plans for assessment are listed in the lesson plan.

Classroom video
- Teacher moves back to a student that the aide had been working with. T: All right, friend. So you take your post-it notes. Take your post-it notes. So here is farmers. (Teacher points to screen.) We are going to find t-t-tools. Which one is t-t-tools? Student points: Here.
- T: Tools. This one is tools, good. So we're gonna click on tools. So I want you to push this button on here and it will read to you information, OK? Ready? All right, go ahead. Student clicks on screen and computer voice reads information about farmers.
- T: Did you hear that? Did you already have tractors? They use tractors. And then they said something called a combine. This is a combine.
- Teacher continues to move from table to table, talking with students as they work, asking them what they are doing, if they are following directions, etc., then moves to another group
- After students move to carpet, teacher asks if anyone has a new fact that they found out about today. Nearly all students raise a hand, and teacher listens to several responses.

Record of Evidence

Cluster 5:   Successful Learning by All Students

Evidence (cont'd.)

Teacher commentary
- Most children in kindergarten cannot read, so teacher selected books that are picture-rich. Student who couldn't' read could see the pictures ("visual literacy piece").
- In the future, they will cover where the professional works, what they do in their job, and any additional information that is interesting.
- T: I have been impressed on a daily basis with what they are writing, but particularly today with the student who used phonetic sounds and identified a ladder for the firemen. That's what delights me. I get to see how much they are growing and helping each other grow because they are pushing each other to use all of their letter sounds.
- Nonfiction lends itself to children who are in kindergarten, whether they are below or above grade level. Children above can read more of the text and can interact with the text like adults interact with the text. It's nice to be able to have the same text with 2 children who are at different levels, because they can both get something out of the text.

Interpretation

- Information is generic in nature, (e.g., there is no identification of the ELL students or the students on an IEP).

- The teacher spends extra time one-on-one with a student who is having difficulty. She uses the computer and practices phonetically with him to help him find the tools for his project.

- Ms. Pierce is concerned that students are doing the work, but not necessarily that they are learning.

- The teacher describes future lessons.

Record of Evidence

Cluster 6: Professionalism

Guiding Questions

- *To what extent does the teacher engage with the professional community (within the school and beyond) and demonstrate a commitment to ongoing professional learning?*

- *Does the teacher collaborate productively with colleagues and contribute to the life of the school?*

- *Does the teacher engage in professional learning and take a leadership role in the school to promote the welfare of students?*

Evidence

No evidence of Cluster 6 is present in this Instructional Set.

Looking at Teaching Through the Lens of the FFT Clusters

A Study Guide for Teacher Learning Communities

Teacher: Sorio
Subject: Math
Grade: 9
Topic: System of Linear Equations

Welcome to the Study Guide for the Sorio Mathematics Instructional Set, a collection of artifacts and videos for an instructional lesson. This Study Guide provides information and instructions on how to examine teaching and learning through the lens of the Framework for Teaching (FFT) Clusters. In order to complete the steps in this Guide, you will need access to the teacher's planning documents, the lesson video, and the teacher commentary video (http://www.danielsongroup.org/study-guides/). Steps 1–5 of this Study Guide focus on examining the Instructional Set and can be done by an individual. Step 6 is a group activity and focuses on sharing results of the analysis and applications of learning.

Step 1 - Lesson Overview

Read the background information of the lesson provided below.

The goal for Ms. Sorio's ninth grade algebra class is for students to be able to solve systems of linear equations in two variables. The class is made up of 8 high-functioning special education students, all of whom have targeted IEP goals for mathematics. Ms. Sorio sets high expectations for the group, saying in her commentary, "They deserve to learn whatever the other students in regular ed are learning right now." In past lessons, students learned that equations with 2 variables can be represented using an ordered pair. Students also have experience solving equations.

The lesson begins with a review of graphing linear equations. Ms. Sorio has written on the board: $y - .25x = 2$. A volunteer student reads the equation for the class, and Ms. Sorio explains that in order to solve the equation, it must be in slope intercept form. [Slope intercept form is represented by y = mx + b, where m is the slope and b equals the y-intercept.] She explains that .25x must be added to each side of the equation, resulting in y = .25x + 2. Ms. Sorio then goes on to show how the equation can be graphed, creating a function table with 3 different values for x, the solutions to the equation, and the resulting ordered pairs.

x =	y =	Ordered Pair
	0.25x + 2	(x, y)
2	.5 + 2 = 2.5	(2, 2.5)
3	.75 + 2 = 2.75	(3, 2.75)
4	1.0 + 2 = 3.0	(4, 3)

As Ms. Sorio leads the class through this explanation, she invites students to help fill in the function table. Maurice struggles with his answer and he is helped by Alberto. Leading the students step-by-step through the procedure, Jason is able to solve the equation and write the ordered pair when the value of x is 4.

Ms. Sorio next leads the students through the steps for graphing the ordered pairs they have just created. Again, she enlists the help of a student. Angel comes to the board first. He hesitates, but marks the coordinates correctly: 2 and 2.5. Other students help plot the points for the remaining two sets of coordinates and Ms. Sorio shows them how the points can be connected to form a straight line. She reinforces the fact that the line represents y = .25x + 2.

"Next," she explains, "we're going to work on a system of linear equations." She explains that a system of linear equations is a collection of 2 or more equations with the same set of unknowns. She leads the class through an activity in which, given four equations, they are to find the two that have the same set of unknowns. Alberto is able to correctly identify the two that have the same set of variables. She explains that both will have the same value for x and y.

Ms. Sorio leads the students step-by-step through the procedure to solve this kind of equation. She explains that the equations first must be written in slope intercept form, or y = mx + b. The second step is to create a function table naming the ordered pairs for each equation. The third step is to graph the lines. The final step is to find the intersection of the two lines.

As Ms. Sorio models the four-step procedure, she invites Alberto to come up and point out the intersection. He does so successfully, and she shows the class how to determine the coordinates for that point. "You get the x and you get the y. This will be the solution of that system of equations."

Ms. Sorio leads the class through an example using a real-life situation as the final activity. The example scenario is: A student saves either a one-dollar bill or a five-dollar bill each day. The student is able to save 25 bills in a month's time, and has a total of $45.00. How many one dollar bills does the student have and how many five dollar bills?

Ms. Sorio explains that x will be the number of one-dollar bills saved and that y will be the number of five-dollar bills saved. Because it takes five single dollars bills to make one five-dollar bill, we can make two equations. First x + y = 25. Second, x + 5y = 45. Ms. Sorio leads the class through the four-step procedure, first for x + y = 25 and then for x + 5y = 45, writing the equations in slope intercept form and then creating the function table.

Students are called on as she leads them through filling in the function chart. One student becomes frustrated and is physically calmed down by the aide.

x =	y =	y =	Ordered Pairs	
x	25 – x	9 – x/5	(x, y)	(x, y)
0	25	9	(0, 25)	(0, 9)
10	25 – 10 or 15	7	(10, 15)	(10, 7)
25	0	4	(25, 0)	(25, 4)

Another student is off task and needs to be refocused. Ms. Sorio moves to quickly finish filling in the table. "Let's do this quick." She and the class plot the points on the graph and she connects the dots to form lines. Students are invited to come up to the board to find the point of intersection. A couple of students struggle with finding the intersection; finally Anthony is able to do so. Ms. Sorio ends the lesson by summarizing that the point of intersection is the solution: x is 20 and y is 5. So, the student saved up 20 one-dollar bills and 5 five-dollar bills, adding up to the $45 dollar total savings

Step 2 - Preparation and Questions

- *Read the teacher's lesson plan and jot down things you expect to see and what you want to look for in the video of the lesson.*

- *Write down any questions or comments you have about the lesson plan.*

Step 3 – Viewing the Classroom Video

- *View the complete video, noting those things you expected to see based on the lesson plan. Also note what was missing based on your expectations from the lesson plan. Jot down significant behaviors by the teacher and students pertinent to the FFT Clusters.*

Step 4 – Selected Highlights of the Lesson Video

Read the highlights of the lesson provided below. Note those matching your highlights of the lesson. For each set of statements, determine the FFT Cluster that is best related to the behaviors presented.

In this lesson, Ms. Sorio explains and models the procedure for graphing linear equations and for graphing a system of linear equations. As she models the procedures, she moves step-by-step sequentially through the process, inviting students to perform a step of the procedure or to give an answer to a calculation she is performing

> A. The teacher has created a safe environment in which no student is hesitant to answer or to volunteer. Interactions between the teacher and the students are caring and supportive. When students working at the board struggle, classmates readily volunteer to help. (Cluster ___)
>
> B. One student, Koron, becomes visibly frustrated, rocking in his chair, speaking rapidly, and waving his arms. "This is hard," he remarks. He is calmed down by the teacher's comments, with assistance from the teacher paraprofessional. (Cluster ___)

C. Student behavior during the lesson is almost entirely appropriate, with only one minor instance of off-task behavior, when Malaki needs to be gently reminded to refocus. (Cluster ___)

D. Students frequently raise their hands to speak and to volunteer, though not always. The teacher does not correct "shouting out," but this does not distract from the lesson. The teacher appears to welcome this engagement rather than discourage it. (Cluster ___)

E. The teacher models the procedures for both parts of the lesson, which is appropriate for teaching procedural knowledge in mathematics. As she moves through the steps, she invites students to answer questions about what goes next, and they are correct for the most part. The teacher indicates that students will be engaged later in guided practice (rehearsal) and independent practice. (Cluster ___)

F. The teacher uses academic language correctly (linear equation, variable, unknown, etc.). The students are not heard using academic language. (Cluster ___)

Step 5 – Viewing the Teacher Commentary

Watch the video of the teacher's commentary about the lesson and jot down any questions or comments you have about the commentary. Read the highlights below and identify the related FFT Cluster.

> A. The teacher explains that the class will learn to solve linear equations with two variables, x and y, by creating graphs. When they have met this goal, they will learn two other ways to find the solution, by elimination and by substitution. (Cluster ___)
>
> B. The teacher states, "They deserve to learn whatever the students in the regular ed classes are learning." (Cluster ___)

Step 6 – Questions, Applications, and Discussion

The purpose of this step is to prompt your analysis and reflection of the Instructional Set and to have you think about applications to your own practice.

1. **Teaching and Learning Related to the FFT Clusters**

The purpose of the activity is to increase your understanding of the relationship between the highlights of the Instructional Set and the FFT Clusters. Your identification of an FFT Cluster for each of the highlights is compared to the Cluster identified by the master coders. The Answer Key is located at the end of the activities. You have options on how to complete the comparison. Determine what might work best for your group's learning. Options include, but are not limited to the following.

- Look at the first set of highlights. Take a poll of what each group member identified as the related FFT Cluster. If all members said the same FFT Cluster, have one or two members say why. Compare the group's response to the answer sheet. Repeat for the remainder of the highlights.

OR

- Have each member take one or two highlights. State the correct answer for each one, and a reason why the highlight demonstrates that FFT Cluster. The member will facilitate a discussion if others had different responses, with the goal of having all understand the justification of the correct answer.

OR

- Have members check their own responses to all the highlights. If there are any incorrect answers, then the member selects one highlight and leads a discussion with the group to learn why others think the highlight matches the correct FFT Cluster.

OR

- Determine your own process to check and discuss the match between highlights and the FFT Clusters.

2. **Analysis and Reflection of the Instructional Set**

The purpose of this activity is for you to analyze and reflect on what you saw and heard in the artifacts and videos, to share your analysis with your peers, and to discuss some of the questions or comments you noted. Review the notes, comments, and questions you recorded when you examined the Instructional Set.

- Identify a key teaching and learning attribute demonstrated in the Instructional Set that was effective and state why you think it worked well.

- Identify a different attribute and provide ideas about how it could be enhanced or improved.

- Share your statements with your group and have your peers react to and build upon your analysis and ideas.

Sample statements:

I noticed that the teacher invited students to become intellectually engaged as she led them through the procedure for solving linear equations. When they were at the board, she prompted them when they struggled, and other students jumped in to help as well. I didn't notice any conversations going on among students in their groups. Since many of the students were very articulate, I wonder if she could use the skills of those students to advance the skills of those who are struggling. I'm also wondering if some students can engage effectively in conversations with their peers to reach a more complete understanding of the concepts. I think that there are a couple of students in the class who could serve as group leaders. Or when paired appropriately, I think they could do a "turn and talk to your neighbor" activity. I'm wondering how that might go.

Additional ideas for statements:

- Degree to which students take pride in their work and demonstrate a commitment to mastering challenging content

- Extent to which the instructional strategies used by the teacher are appropriate for the discipline

- Extent to which students monitor their own learning and provide feedback to others

- Extent to which the teacher provides wait time following questions, allowing students time to think and to construct an answer

3. **Notice, Learn, and Apply**

The purpose of this activity is for you to reflect on what you learned from your analysis of the Instructional Set and to determine how you will apply it to your teaching.

- Complete the statements:
  "I noticed _____."
  (Insert one thing you noticed about the teacher or students.)

  "And I learned _____."
  (State what you learned related to what you noticed.)

  "I will apply what I learned by _____."
  (Provide example of how you will use what you learned in your own context.)

- Share your statements with your group. Have others react and add how they might apply what you noticed to their own teaching context.

Sample statement:

- I noticed that the teacher had the students participate in providing answers, solving equations, and suggesting values for variables.

- I learned that the students in this class are functioning at a high level.

- I have a couple of students in my classroom for whom I'm afraid that I have set expectations too low. I will apply what I've learned by challenging them more, to see if there are ways I can elevate their achievement.

Study Guide for Teachers Answer Key

Highlights from the Lesson Video (Step 4)

A. The teacher has created a safe environment in which no student is hesitant to answer or to volunteer. Interactions between the teacher and the students are caring and supportive. When students working at the board struggle, classmates readily volunteer to help. (Cluster 2 Safe, Respectful, Supportive, and Challenging Learning Environment)

B. One student, Koron, becomes visibly frustrated, rocking in his chair, speaking rapidly, and waving his arms. "This is hard," he remarks. He is calmed down by the teacher's comments, with assistance from the teacher paraprofessional. (Cluster 2 Safe, Respectful, Supportive, and Challenging Learning Environment)

C. Student behavior during the lesson is almost entirely appropriate, with only one minor instance of off-task behavior, when Malaki needs to be gently reminded to refocus. (Cluster 3 Classroom Management)

D. Students frequently raise their hands to speak and to volunteer, though not always. The teacher does not correct "shouting out," but this does not distract from the lesson. The teacher appears to welcome this engagement rather than discourage it. (Cluster 3 Classroom Management)

E. The teacher models the procedures for both parts of the lesson, which is appropriate for teaching procedural knowledge in mathematics. As she moves through the steps, she invites students to answer questions about what goes next, and they are correct for the most part. The teacher indicates that students will be engaged later in guided practice (rehearsal) and independent practice. (Cluster 4 Student Intellectual Engagement)

F. The teacher uses academic language correctly (linear equation, variable, unknown, etc.). The students are not heard using academic language. (Cluster 4 Student Intellectual Engagement)

Study Guide for Teachers Answer Key

Highlights from the Teacher Commentary (Step 5)

A. The teacher explains that the class will learn to solve linear equations with two variables, x and y, by creating graphs. When they have met this goal, they will learn two other ways to find the solution, by elimination and by substitution. (Cluster 1 Clarity of Instructional Purpose and Accuracy of Content)

B. The teacher states, "They deserve to learn whatever the students in the regular ed classes are learning." (Cluster 5 Successful Learning by All Students)

Looking at Teaching Through the Lens of the FFT Clusters

A Study Guide for
Instructional Coach
Learning Communities

Teacher: Sorio
Subject: Math
Grade: 9
Topic: System of Linear Equations

Welcome to the Study Guide for the Sorio Mathematics Instructional Set, a collection of artifacts and videos for an instructional lesson. This Study Guide provides information and instructions on how to examine teaching and learning through the lens of the Framework for Teaching (FFT) Clusters. In order to complete the steps in this Guide, you will need access to the teacher's planning documents, the lesson video, and the teacher commentary video (http://www.danielsongroup.org/study-guides/). Steps 1–5 of this Study Guide focus on examining the Instructional Set and can be done by an individual. Step 6 is a group activity and focuses on sharing results of the analysis and applications of learning.

Step 1 - Lesson Overview

Read the background information of the lesson provided below.

The goal for Ms. Sorio's ninth grade algebra class is for students to be able to solve systems of linear equations in two variables. The class is made up of 8 high-functioning special education students, all of whom have targeted IEP goals for mathematics. Ms. Sorio sets high expectations for the group, saying in her commentary, "They deserve to learn whatever the other students in regular ed are learning right now." In past lessons, students learned that equations with 2 variables can be represented using an ordered pair. Students also have experience solving equations.

The lesson begins with a review of graphing linear equations. Ms. Sorio has written on the board: $y - .25x = 2$. A volunteer student reads the equation for the class, and Ms. Sorio explains that in order to solve the equation, it must be in slope intercept form. [Slope intercept form is represented by y = mx + b, where m is the slope and b equals the y-intercept.] She explains that .25x must be added to each side of the equation, resulting in y = .25x + 2. Ms. Sorio then goes on to show how the equation can be graphed, creating a function table with 3 different values for x, the solutions to the equation, and the resulting ordered pairs.

x =	y =	Ordered Pair
	0.25x + 2	(x, y)
2	.5 + 2 = 2.5	(2, 2.5)
3	.75 + 2 = 2.75	(3, 2.75)
4	1.0 + 2 = 3.0	(4, 3)

As Ms. Sorio leads the class through this explanation, she invites students to help fill in the function table. Maurice struggles with his answer and he is helped by Alberto. Leading the students step-by-step through the procedure, Jason is able to solve the equation and write the ordered pair when the value of x is 4.

Ms. Sorio next leads the students through the steps for graphing the ordered pairs they have just created. Again, she enlists the help of a student. Angel comes to the board first. He hesitates, but marks the coordinates correctly: 2 and 2.5. Other students help plot the points for the remaining two sets of coordinates and Ms. Sorio shows them how the points can be connected to form a straight line. She reinforces the fact that the line represents y = .25x + 2.

"Next," she explains, "we're going to work on a system of linear equations." She explains that a system of linear equations is a collection of 2 or more equations with the same set of unknowns. She leads the class through an activity in which, given four equations, they are to find the two that have the same set of unknowns. Alberto is able to correctly identify the two that have the same set of variables. She explains that both will have the same value for x and y.

Ms. Sorio leads the students step-by-step through the procedure to solve this kind of equation. She explains that the equations first must be written in slope intercept form, or y = mx + b. The second step is to create a function table naming the ordered pairs for each equation. The third step is to graph the lines. The final step is to find the intersection of the two lines.

As Ms. Sorio models the four-step procedure, she invites Alberto to come up and point out the intersection. He does so successfully, and she shows the class how to determine the coordinates for that point. "You get the x and you get the y. This will be the solution of that system of equations."

Ms. Sorio leads the class through an example using a real-life situation as the final activity. The example scenario is: A student saves either a one-dollar bill or a five-dollar bill each day. The student is able to save 25 bills in a month's time, and has a total of $45.00. How many one dollar bills does the student have and how many five dollar bills?

Ms. Sorio explains that x will be the number of one-dollar bills saved and that y will be the number of five-dollar bills saved. Because it takes five single dollars bills to make one five-dollar bill, we can make two equations. First x + y = 25. Second, x + 5y = 45. Ms. Sorio leads the class through the four-step procedure, first for x + y = 25 and then for x + 5y = 45, writing the equations in slope intercept form and then creating the function table.

Students are called on as she leads them through filling in the function chart. One student becomes frustrated and is physically calmed down by the aide.

x =	y =	y =	Ordered Pairs	
x	25 – x	9 – x/5	(x, y)	(x, y)
0	25	9	(0, 25)	(0, 9)
10	25 – 10 or 15	7	(10, 15)	(10, 7)
25	0	4	(25, 0)	(25, 4)

Another student is off task and needs to be refocused. Ms. Sorio moves to quickly finish filling in the table. "Let's do this quick." She and the class plot the points on the graph and she connects the dots to form lines. Students are invited to come up to the board to find the point of intersection. A couple of students struggle with finding the intersection; finally Anthony is able to do so. Ms. Sorio ends the lesson by summarizing that the point of intersection is the solution: x is 20 and y is 5. So, the student saved up 20 one-dollar bills and 5 five-dollar bills, adding up to the $45 dollar total savings

Step 2 - Preparation and Questions

- *Read the teacher's lesson plan and jot down things you expect to see and what you want to look for in the video of the lesson.*

- *Write down any questions or comments you have about the lesson plan.*

Step 3 – Viewing the Classroom Video

- *View the complete video, noting those things you expected to see based on the lesson plan. Also note what was missing based on your expectations from the lesson plan. Jot down significant behaviors by the teacher and students pertinent to the FFT Clusters.*

Step 4 – Selected Highlights of the Lesson Video

Read the highlights of the lesson provided below. Note those matching your highlights of the lesson. For each set of statements, determine the FFT Cluster that is best related to the behaviors presented.

In this lesson, Ms. Sorio explains and models the procedure for graphing linear equations and for graphing a system of linear equations. As she models the procedures, she moves step-by-step sequentially through the process, inviting students to perform a step of the procedure or to give an answer to a calculation she is performing

> A. *The teacher has created a safe environment in which no student is hesitant to answer or to volunteer. Interactions between the teacher and the students are caring and supportive. When students working at the board struggle, classmates readily volunteer to help.* (Cluster ___)
>
> B. *One student, Koron, becomes visibly frustrated, rocking in his chair, speaking rapidly, and waving his arms. "This is hard," he remarks. He is calmed down by the teacher's comments, with assistance from the teacher paraprofessional.* (Cluster ___)

C. *Student behavior during the lesson is almost entirely appropriate, with only one minor instance of off-task behavior, when Malaki needs to be gently reminded to refocus. (Cluster ___)*

D. *Students frequently raise their hands to speak and to volunteer, though not always. The teacher does not correct "shouting out," but this does not distract from the lesson. The teacher appears to welcome this engagement rather than discourage it. (Cluster ___)*

E. *The teacher models the procedures for both parts of the lesson, which is appropriate for teaching procedural knowledge in mathematics. As she moves through the steps, she invites students to answer questions about what goes next, and they are correct for the most part. The teacher indicates that students will be engaged later in guided practice (rehearsal) and independent practice. (Cluster ___)*

F. *The teacher uses academic language correctly (linear equation, variable, unknown, etc.). The students are not heard using academic language. (Cluster ___)*

Step 5 – Viewing the Teacher Commentary

Watch the video of the teacher's commentary about the lesson and jot down any questions or comments you have about the commentary. Read the highlights below and identify the related FFT Cluster.

> A. The teacher explains that the class will learn to solve linear equations with two variables, x and y, by creating graphs. When they have met this goal, they will learn two other ways to find the solution, by elimination and by substitution. (Cluster ___)
>
> B. The teacher states, "They deserve to learn whatever the students in the regular ed classes are learning." (Cluster ___)

Step 6 – Questions, Applications, and Discussion

The purpose of this step is to prompt your analysis and reflection of the Instructional Set and to have you think about applications to your own practice.

1. **Teaching and Learning Related to the FFT Clusters**

The purpose of the activity is to increase your understanding of the relationship between the highlights of the Instructional Set and the FFT Clusters. Your identification of an FFT Cluster for each of the highlights is compared to the Cluster identified by the master coders. The Answer Key is located at the end of the activities. You have options on how to complete the comparison. Determine what might work best for your group's learning. Options include, but are not limited to the following.

- Look at the first set of highlights. Take a poll of what each group member identified as the related FFT Cluster. If all members said the same FFT Cluster, then have one or two members say why. Compare the group's response to the answer sheet. Repeat for the remainder of the sets of highlights.

OR

- Have each member take one or two sets of highlights and be the discussant for them. The discussant will state the correct answer and state a reason why the statements in the set demonstrate the FFT Cluster. The discussant will facilitate a discussion if members had different responses with the goal of all understanding the justification of the correct answer.

OR

- Have members check their own responses to all the sets of highlights. If there are any incorrect answers, then the member selects one set and leads a discussion with the group to learn why others think the highlights match the correct FFT Cluster.

OR

- Determine your own process to check and discuss the match between highlights and the FFT Clusters.

2. **Analysis and Reflection of the Instructional Set**

The purpose of this activity is for you to analyze and reflect on what you saw and heard in the artifacts and videos and to discuss some of the questions or comments you noted. One element of a professional conversation is asking questions to ascertain more information about a teacher's thinking and the behaviors of both students and teacher. This activity allows you and your peers to practice preparing such questions. Your peers can comment on whether your questions are appropriate and will obtain useful information without making the featured teacher feel uneasy or criticized.

The second part of this activity focuses on helping teachers move their practice forward. Please note that having you prepare for and model an entire conversation about the lesson with the featured teacher is not the purpose of this activity as written. Your group can modify or replace the activity to meet your group's needs

- Review the notes, comments, and questions you recorded when you examined the Instructional Set. Pretend you have the opportunity to ask the teacher some questions to get additional information about the strategies used or decisions made for this Instructional Set.

- Share with your group just the questions you would use with the teacher to elicit additional information. Have your peers comment about your questions and add other questions they had about the same event.

- Share with others in your group what you would do to prompt the teacher's thinking and actions to enhance his/her practice. Take turns sharing and discussing the prompts.

Sample A, Part I:

Not being a special education teacher myself, I'm curious to know more about your statement that the students in this class deserve to learn whatever students in the regular education classes are learning. I totally agree with that. Given that the students in this class are cognitively challenged in some ways, what modifications do you make, both in your instruction and in the resources you use, to enable them to perform these skills?

Sample A, Part II:

I noticed that one of the IEP goals was for the students to be able to perform the skills without prompting. Tell me about the degree to which students in your class have met this level of automaticity. Have you had an opportunity to participate in any of the math professional learning events at the SE resource center? I see that you have very high expectations for this group of students and I think the resource center has some excellent resources to help you move them along.

Sample B, Part I:

You gave the students a real life example using linear equations: how many bills would someone end up with if they had saved $45 dollars in ones and fives. It gives students a concrete, authentic experience to relate to. What other authentic applications of linear equations might interest this group of students? How might you find additional examples? Which students in your class might be successful if they were asked to create scenarios that could be solved with linear equations?

Sample B, Part II:

I noticed that you divided your class into two groups for differentiation. What things did you take into consideration when you made the divisions? From the work samples you provided, I see that students in the two groups were given a different assignment. Tell me about the level of support students required as they worked on this assignment. What differences in the type of support did you and your paraprofessional need to provide? Which students in your class might be able to help other students? Perhaps students in the higher group might assist students in the lower group. What are your ideas?

3. **Notice, Learn, and Apply**

The purpose of this activity is for you to reflect on what you learned from your analysis of the Instructional Set and to determine how you will apply it to your teaching.

- Complete the statements:
  "I noticed _____."
  (Insert one thing you noticed about the teacher or students.)

  "And I learned _____."
  (State what you learned related to what you noticed.)

  "I will apply what I learned by _____."
  (Provide example of how you will use what you learned in your own context.)

- Share your statements with your group. Have others react and add how they might apply what you noticed to their own coaching context.

Sample statements:

- I noticed that the paraprofessional moved quickly to the aid of the student who became anxious and frustrated during class. I noticed, too, that she moved to assist the student without prompting from the teacher.

- I learned that paraprofessionals can provide valuable assistance to the teacher, and can do so without being asked by the teacher. In many classrooms I see teacher aides who appear to be waiting on the teacher to ask them to do something. I know it's because they know the teacher is being observed and they want him or her to have the limelight.

- I will apply what I learned by letting teachers know that the performance of the teacher aide reflects on the performance of the teacher, to some degree. In this instance, I can see that the paraprofessional has been well trained, and that there is a level of trust between her and the teacher.

Study Guide for Instructional Coaches Answer Key
Highlights from the Lesson Video (Step 4)

A. The teacher has created a safe environment in which no student is hesitant to answer or to volunteer. Interactions between the teacher and the students are caring and supportive. When students working at the board struggle, classmates readily volunteer to help. (Cluster 2 Safe, Respectful, Supportive, and Challenging Learning Environment)

B. One student, Koron, becomes visibly frustrated, rocking in his chair, speaking rapidly, and waving his arms. "This is hard," he remarks. He is calmed down by the teacher's comments, with assistance from the teacher paraprofessional. (Cluster 2 Safe, Respectful, Supportive, and Challenging Learning Environment)

C. Student behavior during the lesson is almost entirely appropriate, with only one minor instance of off-task behavior, when Malaki needs to be gently reminded to refocus. (Cluster 3 Classroom Management)

D. Students frequently raise their hands to speak and to volunteer, though not always. The teacher does not correct "shouting out," but this does not distract from the lesson. The teacher appears to welcome this engagement rather than discourage it. (Cluster 3 Classroom Management)

E. The teacher models the procedures for both parts of the lesson, which is appropriate for teaching procedural knowledge in mathematics. As she moves through the steps, she invites students to answer questions about what goes next, and they are correct for the most part. The teacher indicates that students will be engaged later in guided practice (rehearsal) and independent practice. (Cluster 4 Student Intellectual Engagement)

F. The teacher uses academic language correctly (linear equation, variable, unknown, etc.). The students are not heard using academic language. (Cluster 4 Student Intellectual Engagement)

Study Guide for Instructional Coaches Answer Key
Highlights from the Teacher Commentary (Step 5)

A. The teacher explains that the class will learn to solve linear equations with two variables, x and y, by creating graphs. When they have met this goal, they will learn two other ways to find the solution, by elimination and by substitution. (Cluster 1 Clarity of Instructional Purpose and Accuracy of Content)

B. The teacher states, "They deserve to learn whatever the students in the regular ed classes are learning." (Cluster 5 Successful Learning by All Students)

Record of Evidence

This Record of Evidence (ROE) contains key evidence aligned to the FFT Clusters. Interpretive statements about the evidence are also provided. The ROE was created by two master coders who recorded evidence and interpretation statements independently, reviewed each others' work, and arrived at a final composite version based on their professional conversations. This version was reviewed by a leader of the master coders. The ROE is included in this Study Guide so users can see what master coders identified as key evidence, and their interpretation of that evidence through the lens of the FFT Clusters. It is provided as an example of one type of analysis of an Instructional Set. The ROEs were created for professional development rather than evaluative purposes. Users are cautioned about using them for teacher evaluation.

Rubric:	Generic
Grade:	9
Subject:	Math
Topic:	System of Linear Equations
Teacher description:	Asian female, unknown experience
Class description:	8 special education students; teacher is assisted by a paraprofessional
Artifacts:	• Lesson plan • Student work
Length of video:	47:28

Record of Evidence

Cluster 1: Clarity of Instructional Purpose and Accuracy of Content

Guiding Questions

- *To what extent does the teacher demonstrate depth of important content knowledge and conduct the class with a clear and ambitious purpose, reflective of the standards for the discipline and appropriate to the students' levels of knowledge and skill?*
- *To what degree are the elements of a lesson (the sequence of topics, instructional strategies, and materials and resources) well designed and executed, and aligned with the purpose of the lesson?*
- *To what extent are they designed to engage students in high-level learning in the discipline?*

Evidence

Instructional Plan

- The teacher's lesson for solving systems of linear equations by graphing is correlated to four math Common Core State Standards (CCSS): model with mathematics, use appropriate tools strategically, attend to precision, and look for and make use of structure. The teacher lists three objectives for the students:
  1. Student will graph linear equations.
  2. Students will find a point that is a solution to create a system of linear equations.
  3. Students will check if equation is true.
- Three vocabulary terms are listed: "intersection," "solution," and "systems of linear equations."
- The teacher also lists four IEP goals for the students:
  1. Students will increase vocabulary/operational skills.
  2. Students will gain effective teamwork skills.
  3. Students will improve listening skills.
  4. Students will attend to task with/without prompt.
- The plan indicates that the lesson will begin with a review of graphing linear equations.
- Lesson Plan (LP): In our past lessons, we have learned that equations with 2 variables can be represented using ordered pair. And all the solutions to that equation are called the solution set. Today we will use that knowledge in order to solve a group of linear equations, but first let us review how to graph the linear equations.

Record of Evidence

Cluster 1: **Clarity of Instructional Purpose and Accuracy of Content**

Evidence (cont'd.)

- The teacher states that she will distribute a review activity and then call for a student to show his/her response.
- The teacher will move on to new material after the review. New material is defining a system of equations.
- LP: Today we will learn about solving systems of linear equations by graphing.
- The teacher will explain this concept and then show a sample graph on the board.
- The next activity will be differentiated for two groups: Group B and Group C. B will solve an equation: $y = 0.25x + 8$. C will solve: $S = 5n$.
- The plan outlines the steps Ms. Sorio will show in order to explain this concept to the students.
- Students will be given graphing paper and a pair of equations (differentiated for the two groups) to graph as guided practice.
- To check for understanding, the teacher will ask the students questions to be answered through individual writing pad. She lists three questions:
  1. Which graph shows y + 4 (a or b)?
  2. What is the solution to the given system of equations?
  3. Pt (4,5) is a solution to equation a and b. True or false?
- LP: If the student was able to answer the 3 questions, then proceed to independent practice. If not, give more guided practice.
- The teacher has planned a worksheet for independent practice.
- A closing performance/summary task is planned where students will sum up the steps in solving systems of equations by graphing.
- The teacher has included a Student Checklist in which she details the skills involved in graphing linear equations. She has each student's name listed so she can check off if the student has the skills.

Teacher Commentary (quotes)

- They have worked on linear equations; they have learned how to graph. Today, they'll be able to solve for the variables x and y given the two equations by graphing. The next step, once they can solve it, we will work on "elimination." Then by substitution.
- The standard is about solving linear equations in two variables. The way I want to break down the lesson is for them to first work on one linear equation and then prepare them how to graph, when we did it before. The solution in this standard is for graphing, the first method of solving the

Record of Evidence

Cluster 1: **Clarity of Instructional Purpose and Accuracy of Content**

Evidence (cont'd.)

linear equation in two variable. I taught them step-by-step, scaffolded, working through the function table and finding that point of intersection. The materials are differentiated for the students, depending on their needs.
- Out main goal is: I do, we do, you do. After practice, they try to do it themselves. As much as possible there will be scaffolding, breaking down of some lessons.
- We try to hit that rigor that is expected. They deserve to learn what the general ed is learning right now.

Artifacts
- The teacher includes samples of the guided practice worksheets from: Alberto (75%), Nijm (100%), Koron (100%), M.B. (100%), Angel (100%), AT (100%), Jason (100%), Maurice (100%),

Video
- T: So now we're going to go back to algebra. The teacher goes off camera for about 30 seconds.
- T: Good morning everyone. Today we're going to start with our new lesson. Our aim for today is how to find a solution for a system of linear equations.
- The teacher talks about what they have done in the past.
- T: We will have a short review of graphing linear equations. So we have an example of this equation. Will someone read this equation for me?
- Malaki reads the equation correctly.
- T: So in solving for that, remember what I told you before. We have to switch it into a slope intersect form. We have to separate the variables y and x.
- T: What do we take away from here? Calls on Anthony. S: We add.
- Camera operator pauses the lesson to adjust microphone, etc.
- T: What do we do? Malaki answers.
- T: What do we do on the next side? Angel answers correctly.
- T: What do we do next? The teacher calls on Jason. He answers correctly.
- Ms. Sorio asks for a variable. Koron: I'll take two. T: What do we do with the 2? Someone answers correctly.
- The teacher fills in the equation with the variable 2.
- T: What does that equal? Get your calculators out. A paraprofessional helps Koron.
- Some students call out the answer. Koron: "I got it."

Record of Evidence

Cluster 1:   **Clarity of Instructional Purpose and Accuracy of Content**

Evidence (cont'd.)

- T: Let's have another variable: 3.
- The teacher calls on Maurice to come to the white board. Maurice is writing on board.
- S: I can't see the equation.
- T: Can somebody help Maurice? Malaki: 2.5 (correct). Maurice fills it in.
- T: Who would like to write the ordered pair? The teacher calls on Alberto.
- Alberto begins. T: Remember the x and the y variables. Alberto fills it in correctly.
- T: What did I say, how many points? Student answers correctly, "3." Koron echoes.
- T: Let's have another variable. 4 (Malaki)
- T: So let me write down. Koron what is next? He answers correctly.
- T: Jason do you have an answer? Student answers 3 correctly.
- T: Jason help me out with the order. Jason answers incorrectly. The teacher helps, then he answers correctly.
- T: Let's graph these points. Let's have the first point. Who would like to do the first point?
- Malaki raises hand to volunteer. The teacher calls on Malaki, who comes to the board. He places the point in the wrong place. The teacher cues. Malaki thinks it through out loud and gets it right.
- T: Angel, what do you think? Angel: Yes (can explain why it is correct).
- T: Where is the next point? She calls on Angel to come to the board.
- Angel pauses and answers out loud correctly. He hesitates, and then begins writing. It is correct. T: Thanks, Angel.
- T: Next point. Anthony is called on and comes to the board. Anthony places it correctly. T: Thanks you!
- T: What do we do next? Hands go up. Ss: We connect the points.
- T: What do we have? What do we call this? All students call out correctly.
- T: What equation? A students answers correctly.
- T: Any questions with that? Ss: No.
- T: With our next lesson, we are going to work on a system of linear equations. What is a system of linear equation? If we have one linear equation there, this time, we will be needing more linear equations. When you say a system of linear equations, it will be a collection of two or more equations with the same unknowns.

Record of Evidence

Cluster 1:   **Clarity of Instructional Purpose and Accuracy of Content**

Evidence (cont'd.)

- The teacher calls on students to pick an equation from a choice. She calls on Koron to place one on the board. She then calls on Anthony to put one on the board, then for Malaki to put one on.
- T: Alberto can you put it on the board? What equations here would have the same variables?
- Alberto answers correctly. T: So we put them together.
- T: So we have here two sets of equations. Which one would be considered our system of equations? Same set of unknowns. Alberto: This is the correct pair with the same unknown.
- T: So we will have an example. How do we solve this kind of equation? The teacher models the correct steps. She explains the steps to the students verbally.
- T: Why do we need the function table? Student answers correctly.
- T: These are the basic three steps that we do. Who can define for me what intersection is? She calls on Malaki, who answers correctly. T (cues): They will have a common ___? Malaki fills in "point."
- Ms. Sorio shows the two lines graphed.
- She calls on Alberto to show the point of intersection. He does so correctly.
- T (repeats): This is the point of intersection. She explains how to find the coordinates, which is part of the answer.
- T: OK, so what can we get here? Student answers correctly.
- T (giving an example using dollar bills): OK now, we will have an example. You have twenty-five pieces of bills together and you need to know how many bills are you going to save. X will be the number of one-dollar bills and Y will be the number of five-dollar bills. How many ones in a five-dollar bill. Student answers correctly.
- The teacher shows the equations on the board and explains.
- T: Don't forget the "dollars." You must say the unit or it will have no meaning.
- She moves through the problem, interjecting questions that students answer correctly.
- Ms. Sorio calls on Maurice. He answers correctly. T: Can you see it from there?
- She continues showing the solution to the problem.
- The teacher calls on Angel then Malaki. Malaki explains correctly.
- T: The only way to do that is to…? Students answers correctly, "Divide."

Record of Evidence

Cluster 1:   **Clarity of Instructional Purpose and Accuracy of Content**

Evidence (cont'd.)

- T: What's 45 divided by 5? Students answers correctly.
- T: All right, what's the next step? Students answers correctly, "Use the function table."
- The teacher begins to fill in the function table.
- T: Let's make it easy; let's start with zero. Anthony, what is zero over five? Anthony answers correctly.
- T: Help me out Maurice. What will be the order here? Maurice comes to the board. The teacher offers cues, and Maurice is still struggling. She helps him, and he writes in the correct answer.
- Malaki explains what to do next.
- The teacher chooses the next number, 10, and calls on Jason. T: What's 25 minus ten? He comes to the board and does it correctly.
- Malaki asks for a tissue.
- T: Yes you do know it Jason! He is having difficulty. Students call out to help him.
- T (in a singsong manner): Thank you. Let's go to the next one.
- She calls on Koron. He does not know the answer and gets upset and frustrated. He answers fervently, "It's a ten."
- Paraprofessional touches his hand, then on his back to calm him down.
- T: Koron, thank you for your help.
- Koron: It is hard!! He is still upset a bit. Rocking.
- Malaki is off task and teacher call him out. T: Is that part of our lesson? Malaki: No. They move on.
- S (thinking out loud): so it's nine minus five . . .
- At this point, students call out 4, which is incorrect. T: Is it four? No and puts zero down.
- The teacher moves into the graphing stage of the demonstration. She demonstrates graphing the coordinates for each of the equations. She connects the points to form lines.
- Ms. Sorio now calls on Angel to come to the board and enter the coordinates on the graph. Angel does it correctly.
- Alberto volunteers to put the next ones on the graph. He does so correctly.
- The teacher calls on Malaki. He come to the board and makes the line.
- T: Jason, can you see the lines? Would you like to stand up and look at it?

Record of Evidence

Cluster 1: **Clarity of Instructional Purpose and Accuracy of Content**

Evidence (cont'd.)

- T: Now, where it the point of intersection? She calls on Koron. He comes to the board and tries. Teacher has to show him. T: You did it! (But only after she showed him where to put it.)
- The teacher calls on Jason. She repeats the definition of "Point of Intersection." She shows him. T: Where do they meet? Jason can't figure it out. She asks him to sit down and calls on Anthony. Anthony gets it correct.
- T: Let me just explain this. This red line is equation number 2. This is the other equation. This line is passing through this point. Is this right, Alberto?
- The teacher makes the point again about the point of intersection and shows the point's coordinates.
- T: This is now the solution.
- Vocabulary is posted on bulletin board: "Linear equation," "intersection."

Interpretation

- The instructional purpose and learning tasks of this lesson on graphing linear equations are clear to the students. The information presented by the teacher to the class is accurate and suitable to most students.

- Most of the students provide correct answers throughout the lesson, but Maurice and Koron appear to struggle when called upon. One student does not have a video release form and is not seen or heard on camera.

Record of Evidence

Cluster 2:   Safe, Respectful, Supportive, and Challenging Learning Environment

Guiding Questions

- *To what extent do the interactions between teacher and students, and among students, demonstrate genuine caring and a safe, respectful, supportive, and also challenging learning environment?*

- *Do teachers convey high expectations for student learning and encourage hard work and perseverance? Is the environment safe for risk taking?*

- *Do students take pride in their work and demonstrate a commitment to mastering challenging content?*

Evidence

- The teacher calls on students by name.
- When students working at the white board are not able to provide an answer, the teacher asks the class for help, and they provide the correct answer politely.
- No inappropriate interaction among or between students in observed.
- Students appear comfortable providing answers. Students readily volunteer to come to the white board and share their answers.
- When Koron becomes upset and frustrated, the teacher supports him and the paraprofessional touches his hand and also rubs his back to calm him down. The teacher praises Koron several times.
- Koron gets excited when he is able to get the correct answer. He appears to be a slow processor, and calls out answers that he is able to get even after other students have answered correctly.
- The teacher includes everyone in the class in the lesson and calls on everyone, except for Nijm, who does not have permission to be videotaped.
- When students struggle, the teacher cues them, asking questions that help them come up with the answer.
- The teacher reminds students to use the unit "dollars," and reminds them that numbers have no meaning unless you name the unit.
- The teacher keeps the students cognitively engaged for the entire period by calling on them all throughout the lesson.
- Direct interaction between students is not observed.
- At one point, Koron called out "This is hard."

Record of Evidence

Cluster 2: Safe, Respectful, Supportive, and Challenging Learning Environment

Interpretation

- Interactions between the teacher and the students are caring and supportive. No direct interactions between students is observed, but students responded appropriately by helping others at the white board.
- The teacher has created a safe environment. No students are hesitant to answer or volunteer.
- Students show pride, especially Koron, by shouting out answers they know.
- Koron also shows his frustration with the difficulty of the lesson, but remains engaged.

Record of Evidence

Cluster 3:   Classroom Management
Guiding Questions

- Is the classroom well run and organized?

- Are classroom routines and procedures clear and carried out efficiently by both teacher and students with little loss of instructional time?

- To what extent do students themselves take an active role in their smooth operation?

- Are directions for activities clearly explained so that there is no confusion?

- Do students not only understand and comply with standards of conduct, but also play an active part in setting the tone for maintaining those standards?

- How does the physical environment support the learning activities?

Evidence
- Student behavior during the lesson is almost entirely appropriate, with only one minor instance of off-task behavior when Malaki needs to be gently reminded.
- Students remain in their seats the entire lesson.
- The class consists of eight students and is conducted as a whole group lesson.
- Students frequently, but not always, raise their hands to speak and to volunteer. The teacher does not correct "shouting out," but this does not distract from the lesson; the teacher appears to welcome the engagement rather than discourage it.
- Students do not react when Koron becomes agitated.
- Students come to the white board when called upon to do so by the teacher.
- Students are seated in groups of about three. They can all see the whiteboard, though the teacher does ask Jason twice if he can see the board. At one point she asks if he would like to stand up to see the board.
- The paraprofessional is not seen on camera working with students, but we do see her gently touch Koron's hand and rub his back when he becomes agitated; she does this without prompting from the teacher.

Record of Evidence

Cluster 3:   Classroom Management

Interpretation

- The classroom is well run and organized, with little loss of instructional time. The physical environment supports this whole-class lesson.

- Students take an active role in the smooth operation of the class, following established procedures for volunteering and moving to the whiteboard.

- Students do not react to Koron's agitation. Behavior is entirely appropriate.

- The paraprofessional appears to know what she is supposed to do without instructions from the teacher during the lesson.

Record of Evidence

Cluster 4: Student Intellectual Engagement

Guiding Questions

- To what extent are students intellectually engaged in a classroom of high intellectual energy?
- What is the nature of what students are doing?
- Are they being challenged to think and make connections through both the instructional activities and the questions explored?
- Do the teacher's explanations of content correctly model academic language and invite intellectual work by students?
- Are students asked to explain their thinking, to construct logical arguments citing evidence, and to question the thinking of others?
- Are the instructional strategies used by the teacher suitable to the discipline, and to what extent do they promote student agency in the learning of challenging content?

Evidence

- The teacher leads the class in a review of graphing linear equations in the first part of the lesson. She goes through each of the steps, calling on individual students for answers as she models the procedure. Students consistently provide correct answers.
- She models the procedure for graphing sets of linear equations in the second part of the lesson. She calls upon students to provide answers during her explanation, based on their prior learning. Students for the most part answer correctly.
- The teacher uses academic language correctly (e.g., linear equation, variable, unknown, etc.), but the students are not heard using academic language.
- Students frequently explain their thinking, but they are not often encouraged to challenge the thinking of others. At one point, the teacher asks the class, "Is this correct?"
- The teacher models the procedures for both parts of the lesson, which is appropriate for mathematics instruction. As she moves through the steps, she invites students to answer questions about what goes next, and they are correct for the most part.
- The lesson is modeled by the teacher, but we do not see the students moving through the procedure independently, so we have no evidence that they can do the procedure by themselves.

Record of Evidence

Cluster 4: Student Intellectual Engagement

Interpretation

- Students are highly cognitively engaged at a developmentally appropriate level.
- The activities require the students to recall information from prior lessons and they supply correct answers.
- The teacher uses academic language.
- The teacher leads the students through the procedure for graphing; the students are not observed executing the procedure independently.

Record of Evidence

Cluster 5: Successful Learning by All Students
Guiding Questions

- To what extent does the teacher ensure learning by all students?

- Does the teacher monitor student understanding through specifically designed questions or instructional techniques?

- To what extent do students monitor their own learning and provide respectful feedback to classmates?

- Does the teacher make modifications in presentations or learning activities where necessary, taking into account the degree of student learning?

- Has the teacher sought out other resources (including parents) to support students' learning?

- In reflection, is the teacher aware of the success of the lesson in reaching students?

Evidence
- The class is small and all students are participating. The teacher calls on each student and students frequently volunteer.
- The teacher is able to listen to their answers and watch as they enter information into tables or on the graph. She is able to monitor each student's understanding of the procedure for graphing linear equations.
- Students are not asked or observed to monitor other student's learning, nor to give feedback to other students.
- The teacher has designed an independent practice worksheet that will be used next, but we do not see it in this observation. The teacher provides students' work samples, with all students but one getting 100%. There is no evidence about whether the students did the sample work independently or if they were led through the procedures.

Interpretation

- The teacher ensures developmentally appropriate learning by all students by monitoring their thinking closely and listening to their answers.

- The students do not monitor their own learning nor provide feedback to classmates.

Record of Evidence

Cluster 6: Professionalism

Guiding Questions

- To what extent does the teacher engage with the professional community (within the school and beyond) and demonstrate a commitment to ongoing professional learning?

- Does the teacher collaborate productively with colleagues and contribute to the life of the school?

- Does the teacher engage in professional learning and take a leadership role in the school to promote the welfare of students?

Evidence

No evidence of Cluster 6 is present in this Instructional Set.

Appendix A: The FFT Clusters Study Guide Series Team

Ron Anderson, EdD; OH. Danielson Group Consultant.

Dauna Easley, MEd; OH. University of Cincinnati supervisor for student teachers.

Nancy Flickinger, MEd; OH. National Board Certified (AYA/ELA), Teaching Professions Academy Instructor.

Linda Goodwin, MEd; AR. Arkansas LEADS/TESS Support Consultant, Arkansas School Improvement Specialist, Arkansas Quest Leadership Mentor for Administrators, Danielson Group Consultant.

Bobbie Grice, MEd; OH. Resident Educator Coordinator.

Shirley Hall, MEd; NJ. President, GreenLight for Learning, LLC; Former School and District Administrator, Danielson Group Member.

Donna Hanby, PhD; OH. Educational Consultant (Assessment & Accreditation): Educator Preparation Programs.

Kathleen Hanson, MEd; ID. Hanson Educational Consulting, Danielson Group Consultant.

MaryLou McGirr, MEd; SD. Learning Specialist, Technology & Innovation in Education; Trainer for Cognitive Coaching; Danielson Group Consultant.

Joanie Peterson, MEd; OR. Human Resources/ Professional Development Administrator; Danielson Group Consultant.

Sue Presler, MEd; NE. Training Associate, Thinking Collaborative. Trainer for Cognitive Coaching, Adaptive Schools, and Habits of Mind, Danielson Group Member.

Carol Rauch, EdD; OH. University of Cincinnati supervisor for student teachers and Associate Director of Professional Development; Danielson Group Consultant.

Cynthia M. Tocci, PhD; VA. Educational Observations, LLC, Danielson Group Director of Instructional Design.

Appendix B:
List of Study Guide Sets

Set No.	Subject	Grade
1	ELA	8
1	Math	3
1	Social Studies	11
2	Tech	9
2	ELA	8
2	Math	4
3	Math	9-10
3	ELA	2
3	Social Studies	7
4	ELA	12
4	Math	2
4	Social Studies	9
5	Science	4
5	Math	11
5	ELA	7
6	Math	10
6	ELA	5
6	Math	K
7	Math	6
7	ELA	9
7	Math	1
8	ELA	K
8	ELA	4
8	Math	9

Vision

Each educator and student experiences a safe and inclusive learning environment that promotes joyful inquiry, efficacy, intellectual rigor, and reflection grounded in the Framework for Teaching.

Mission

To advance the principles of the Framework for Teaching by partnering with educators and policy leaders at all levels to strengthen professional practices and promote education policies that elevate teacher development and leadership in service of student learning.

For information about our services, or to download a free copy of the FFT Clusters document, visit our website: www.danielsongroup.org

Made in the USA
Middletown, DE
14 September 2021